THE SALTER AIR FRYER COOKBOOK FOR BEGINNERS

1000+ Days of Super Easy, Flavorful, and Affordable Air Fryer Recipes for Both New and Experienced Users

OPAL N. SNIDER

TABLE OF CONTENTS

INTRODUCTION

My Air Frying Journey

When I first heard about air fryers, I was sceptical. Another kitchen gadget, I thought, destined to gather dust in the cupboard. But when a friend raved about her Salter air fryer, I decided to give it a go. Little did I know it would revolutionise my cooking and set me on a path to creating this very cookbook.

My first attempt was chips - a British classic. As I pulled out the basket, I was gobsmacked. There, nestled inside, were golden, crispy chips that could rival any chippy. The best part? I'd used just a fraction of the oil I normally would. From that moment, I was hooked. Over the next few months, I experimented with everything from crispy chicken to roasted veg. I even managed to whip up a decent Victoria sponge. The air fryer became my go-to for quick weeknight dinners, weekend fry-ups, and even impressing guests at dinner parties.

But it wasn't all smooth sailing. There were plenty of burnt offerings and undercooked disasters along the way. I learned the hard way about the importance of preheating, the magic of a light oil spray, and the transformative power of a good shake mid-cook. As I shared my successes (and failures) with friends and family, I realised I wasn't alone in my air fryer adventures. Many were curious but unsure where to start. Others had air fryers gathering dust, unsure how to use them to their full potential.

That's when the idea for this cookbook was born. I wanted to create a guide that I wish I'd had when I started - something comprehensive yet approachable, packed with tips and tricks, and full of recipes that real people would want to cook and eat. So, whether you're an air fryer novice or looking to expand your repertoire, welcome to the wonderful world of air frying. Trust me, once you start, you'll wonder how you ever managed without it.

WHY CHOOSE A SALTER AIR FRYER?

In the ever-expanding world of air fryers, Salter stands out for several reasons. First and foremost, it's a brand we Brits know and trust. For over 260 years, Salter has been a staple in British kitchens, known for its quality and reliability.

But what sets Salter air fryers apart? Let's break it down:

1. User-Friendly Design: Salter air fryers are intuitive to use, even for complete beginners. The controls are straightforward, and the digital displays are clear and easy to read.

2. Consistent Results: One thing I've noticed with my Salter air fryer is its ability to cook food evenly. No more dishes that are burnt on the outside and raw in the middle.

3. Variety of Sizes: Whether you're cooking for one or feeding a family, Salter has an air fryer to suit your needs. Their range includes compact models perfect for small kitchens, as well as larger ones ideal for big households.

4. Energy Efficiency: In these times of rising energy costs, the Salter air fryer is a godsend. It uses significantly less electricity than a traditional oven, and the cooking times are often shorter too.

5. Easy to Clean: The non-stick coating on Salter air fryer baskets makes them a doddle to clean. Most parts are dishwasher safe too, which is always a bonus in my book.

6. Versatility: From chips to cakes, roasts to risottos, the Salter air fryer can handle it all. It's not just for 'frying' - it can bake, roast, and even reheat leftovers to crispy perfection.

7. Safety Features: With automatic shut-off and cool-touch handles, Salter air fryers prioritise safety, giving you peace of mind in the kitchen.

8. British Customer Support: If you ever run into issues, Salter's UK-based customer service team is on hand to help.

9. Value for Money: While not the cheapest on the market, Salter air fryers offer excellent value for money, balancing quality with affordability.

10. Healthier Cooking: Last but certainly not least, Salter air fryers allow you to enjoy your favourite fried foods with up to 80% less fat. It's a win-win for your taste buds and your waistline. In my experience, investing in a quality air fryer pays off in the long run. And with Salter, you're not just buying an appliance - you're investing in a trusted British brand with a long history of kitchen innovation.

HOW THIS COOKBOOK WILL TRANSFORM YOUR COOKING

Right, let's talk about how this cookbook is going to change the game for you. Whether you're a complete novice in the kitchen or a seasoned cook looking to expand your repertoire, this book is designed to make you an air frying pro in no time.

HERE'S WHAT YOU CAN EXPECT:

1. Comprehensive Guide to Your Salter Air Fryer

We'll start by getting you acquainted with your new kitchen best friend. I'll walk you through every button, feature, and accessory of your Salter air fryer. By the time we're done, you'll know this machine inside out.

2. Air Frying 101

Next, we'll cover the basics of air frying. You'll learn how it works, why it's healthier, and how it compares to traditional cooking methods. We'll also bust some common air-frying myths along the way.

3. Essential Techniques

I'll share all the tips and tricks I've learned on my air frying journey. From preheating to proper food arrangement, these techniques will ensure you get perfect results every time.

4. Troubleshooting Guide

Let's face it, things don't always go to plan in the kitchen. That's why I've included a comprehensive troubleshooting section. Soggy chips? Burnt chicken? We'll tackle common issues and how to solve them.

5. Diverse Recipe Collection

The heart of this cookbook is, of course, the recipes. I've included 150 delicious, family-friendly recipes spread across 10 chapters. From quick breakfasts to impressive dinner party dishes, you'll find something for every occasion.

6. Adapting Your Favourite Recipes

Once you've mastered the basics, I'll show you how to adapt your existing recipes for the air fryer. You'll be amazed at how many of your favourite dishes can be air-fried.

7. Meal Planning and Prep

I've included tips on how to incorporate your air fryer into your weekly meal planning. You'll also find advice on batch cooking and storing air-fried foods.

8. Healthier Alternatives

One of the best things about air frying is the ability to create healthier versions of traditionally fried foods. I'll show you how to make guilt-free versions of your favourite treats.

9. Beyond Frying

Your Salter air fryer isn't just for chips and chicken wings. I'll introduce you to the world of air fryer baking, roasting, and even dehydrating.

10. Resources and References

At the back of the book, you'll find handy reference guides including a temperature conversion chart, ingredient substitutions, and a glossary of cooking terms.

By the time you've worked your way through this cookbook, you'll be air-frying with confidence. You'll have a repertoire of delicious recipes under your belt, and the skills to create your air fryer masterpieces.

But more than that, I hope this cookbook will transform your relationship with cooking. Air frying makes home cooking quicker, easier, and healthier. It opens up a world of culinary possibilities, all at the touch of a button.

Understanding Your Salter Air Fryer

Before we dive into the delicious world of air frying, let's get to know your new kitchen companion. Understanding the ins and outs of your Salter air fryer will set you up for success and help you make the most of this versatile appliance.

PARTS AND FUNCTIONS

When I first unboxed my Salter air fryer, I'll admit I was a bit overwhelmed. But fear not. Once you break it down, it's quite simple. Let's go through each part and its function:

The Main Unit

This is the heart of your air fryer. It houses the heating element and fan, which work together to circulate hot air around your food. The exterior is usually made of durable plastic or stainless steel, designed to stay cool to the touch even when cooking.

The Basket

Ah, the basket - where the magic happens. This removable container is where you'll place your food. It's typically non-stick and perforated to allow hot air to circulate. I've found that giving the basket a light spray of oil before cooking helps prevent sticking and makes cleaning a breeze.

The Drawer

The basket sits inside the drawer, which slides in and out of the main unit. It's designed to catch any drips or crumbs, keeping your air fryer clean. Some models have a button to release the basket from the drawer, which is handy for shaking or turning food mid-cook.

The Heating Element

Located at the top of the main unit, this is what gets your food crispy and golden. It works in tandem with the fan to circulate hot air evenly around your food.

The Fan

This powerful little motor is what sets air fryers apart from conventional ovens. It circulates hot air at high speed, creating that crispy exterior we all love in fried food.

Air Vents

Usually located at the back of the unit, these allow excess hot air to escape. Be sure to keep them unobstructed for optimal performance.

The Power Cord

Simple but essential. Make sure you have a suitable plug socket nearby before setting up your air fryer.

Understanding these parts will help you use your Salter air fryer more effectively. For example, knowing about the perforated basket helped me realise why it's important to shake certain foods during cooking - it ensures even crisping all around.

Remember, your air fryer might look slightly different depending on the model, but these basic components will be present in all Salter air fryers. Get familiar with each part, and you'll be air-frying like a pro in no time.

CONTROL PANEL GUIDE

Now that we've covered the physical parts of your Salter air fryer, let's demystify the control panel. This is where you'll set your cooking time and temperature, and where you can access any preset functions, your model might have.

Power Button

This one's pretty straightforward - it turns your air fryer on and off. Some models require you to press and hold for a few seconds to power on.

Temperature Control

This allows you to set your cooking temperature. Most Salter models let you adjust the temperature in 5°C increments, typically ranging from about 80°C to 200°C. I've found that 180°C is a sweet spot for many recipes, but we'll get into specific temperatures later in the cookbook.

Timer

The timer function lets you set how long you want to cook your food. It usually goes up to 60 minutes. A handy tip: if a recipe calls for longer than 60 minutes, simply restart the timer when it dings.

Start/Pause Button

Use this to begin cooking once you've set your time and temperature. It's also handy for pausing mid-cook if you need to shake or turn your food.

Preset Functions

Depending on your model, you might have preset buttons for common foods like chips, chicken, or fish. These are great starting points, but don't be afraid to adjust times and temperatures to suit your preferences.

Digital Display

This shows your set time and temperature. Some models alternate between displaying time and temperature during cooking.

Preheat Indicator

If your model has a preheat function, this light will let you know when the air fryer has reached the set temperature.

Shake Reminder

Some fancy models have a shake reminder - a beep that tells you when it's time to shake your food for even cooking. If yours doesn't have this, no worries - I'll guide you on when to shake in the recipes.

Getting to grips with the control panel might seem daunting at first, but trust me, it quickly becomes second nature. I remember feeling a bit nervous the first time I used mine, but by the third or fourth use, I was adjusting times and temperatures with confidence. One last tip: don't be afraid to experiment. While the preset functions are useful, you'll often get the best results by tailoring the time and temperature to your specific recipe and preferences.

ACCESSORIES AND THEIR USES

One of the things I love about Salter air fryers is the range of accessories available. These can expand what you can do with your air fryer, taking it from a chip-making machine to a versatile cooking powerhouse. Let's explore some common accessories and how to use them:

Grill Pan

This is brilliant for foods that might drip or stick to the regular basket. I use mine for marinated meats, fish fillets, and even for baking small cakes. The raised ridges give you those lovely char marks too.

Baking Dish

Perfect for dishes with sauces or batters. Think lasagna, frittatas, or even a small Victoria sponge. Just make sure to choose one that fits comfortably in your air fryer basket.

Pizza Pan

Yes, you can make pizza in your air fryer. A perforated pizza pan helps crisp up the base beautifully. I've found it's great for reheating leftover pizza too - it comes out so much better than from the microwave.

Silicone Muffin Cups

These are fantastic for individual portions. I use them for egg cups, mini frittatas, and of course, muffins and cupcakes. They're also much easier to clean than traditional metal muffin tins.

Rack

A rack can be a game-changer, effectively doubling your cooking space. Use it to cook different foods at the same time - just remember that the food on top will cook faster due to its proximity to the heating element.

Oil Sprayer

While not strictly an air fryer accessory, I find an oil sprayer invaluable. It allows you to add just a light coating of oil to your food or the basket, which is often all you need for that perfect crispy finish.

Parchment Liners

These pre-cut liners fit perfectly in your air fryer basket and make cleanup a breeze. They're especially useful for sticky or messy foods. Just be sure to weigh them down with food to prevent them from flying up into the heating element.

Tongs

A good pair of silicone-tipped tongs is essential for safely removing hot food from your air fryer. Look for a pair with long handles to keep your hands away from the heat.

Remember, not all accessories are created equal. Always use accessories that are specifically designed for air fryers, and check that they're compatible with your Salter model. Using the wrong accessories can damage your air fryer or lead to poor cooking results.

I'd recommend starting with the basics - your air fryer basket will be sufficient for most recipes in this book. As you get more comfortable and adventurous with your air frying, you can gradually add accessories to your collection. With these accessories, your Salter air fryer can do so much more than just crispy chips (although it does those brilliantly too.). From baking to grilling, roasting to reheating, your air fryer is truly a jack-of-all-trades in the kitchen. So, let's get cooking.

BENEFITS OF AIR FRYING

Now that we understand how air fryers work, let's talk about why you might want to use one. When I first got my Salter air fryer, I was primarily interested in making healthier versions of fried foods. But I quickly discovered that the benefits of air frying extend far beyond just health. Here are some of the main advantages I've found:

1. Healthier Cooking: This is the big one, and likely why many of us first consider an air fryer. By using hot air instead of hot oil, you can reduce the fat content of your food by up to 80% compared to traditional frying methods. This means you can enjoy your favourite fried foods with significantly fewer calories and less fat. I've found this particularly brilliant for things like chips, chicken wings, and even doughnuts.

2. Time-saving: Air fryers typically cook food faster than conventional ovens. For example, a batch of chips that might take 30 minutes in a regular oven often takes just 15-20 minutes in my air fryer. This is a godsend on busy weeknights when I need to get dinner on the table quickly.

3. Energy Efficient: Because air fryers are smaller and cook food faster than traditional ovens, they use less energy. This is not only good for the environment but can also help reduce your energy bills. Win-win.

4. Easy to Clean: Most air fryer baskets have a non-stick coating and are dishwasher safe. Compare this to the mess of cleaning up after deep frying, and its clear why air fryers are a favourite for those of us who hate washing up.

5. Versatility: While "frying" is in the name, air fryers can do so much more. I use mine for roasting vegetables, baking cakes, reheating leftovers, and even making toast. It's like having a mini oven right on your countertop.

6. No Hot Oil: Deep frying can be dangerous, with the risk of hot oil splashes or spills. Air fryers eliminate this risk, making them a safer option, especially if you have children or pets in the kitchen.

7. Consistent Results: Once you get the hang of your air fryer, you'll find it produces consistent results time after time. No more worrying about oil temperature or uneven cooking.

8. No Lingering Smells: Deep frying can leave your house smelling of oil for days. Air frying, on the other hand, produces minimal odours.

9. Portion Control: The size of the air fryer basket naturally limits how much you can cook at once. While this might seem like a disadvantage, I've found it helpful for portion control.

10. Encourages Home Cooking: Because air frying is so quick and easy, I've found myself cooking at home more often rather than relying on takeaways. This has been great for both my wallet and my waistline.

11. Great for Leftovers: Air fryers are brilliant for reheating leftovers. They bring back the crispy texture that microwaves often destroy. I particularly love using mine to reheat pizza – it comes out with a crispy base and melty cheese, almost like it's fresh from the pizzeria.

12. Perfect for Small Households: If you're cooking for one or two, an air fryer can be more practical than heating a large oven. It's also great for small kitchens where space is at a premium.

Of course, like any cooking method, air frying isn't perfect for everything. You might find that some foods don't come out quite the same as their deep-fried counterparts. And if you're cooking for a large family, you might need to cook in batches.

But for me, the benefits far outweigh any drawbacks. My Salter air fryer has become an indispensable part of my kitchen. It's helped me eat healthier, save time, and even experiment with new recipes. Whether you're looking to cut down on calories, save time in the kitchen, or just try out a new cooking method, I think you'll find air frying a game-changer. So, let's get cooking.

SAFETY PRECAUTIONS

Now, I know safety might not be the most exciting topic, but it's crucial when you're dealing with any kitchen appliance – especially one that gets as hot as an air fryer. Don't worry, using your Salter air fryer is generally very safe, but there are a few precautions to keep in mind to ensure you have a worry-free cooking experience.

1. Read the Manual

I know, I know – nobody likes reading manuals. But trust me, it's worth taking a few minutes to familiarise yourself with your specific model's safety guidelines. Different models might have slightly different recommendations.

2. Use on a Stable, Heat-Resistant Surface

Always place your air fryer on a flat, stable surface that can withstand heat. I learned this the hard way when I once put mine on a plastic tray – not a good idea.

3. Allow for Proper Ventilation

Make sure there's at least 10cm of space around all sides of the air fryer. This allows for proper air circulation and prevents overheating. Don't place it right up against a wall or under cabinets.

4. Keep Away from Water

Like any electrical appliance, your air fryer should be kept away from water. Never immerse the main unit in water, and be careful not to let water get into the electrical components when cleaning.

5. Don't Leave Unattended

While it's tempting to set it and forget it, it's best not to leave your air fryer unattended while it's running. This is especially important if you have curious pets or little ones.

6. Use Oven Mitts

The basket and drawer can get very hot during cooking. Always use oven mitts or heat-resistant gloves when handling these parts. I once grabbed the basket with my bare hands – let's just say I won't be making that mistake again.

7. Be Careful of Steam

When you open the air fryer during or after cooking, be aware that hot steam may escape. Open it away from your face and hands.

8. Don't Overfill

Resist the temptation to cram as much food as possible into the basket. Overfilling can lead to uneven cooking and might even be a fire hazard if food touches the heating element.

9. Avoid Metal Utensils

To protect the non-stick coating on your basket, use wooden, silicone, or plastic utensils. Metal can scratch the surface and reduce its effectiveness.

10. Let It Cool Before Cleaning

Always allow your air fryer to cool completely before attempting to clean it. This prevents any risk of burns and makes cleaning easier too.

11. Check the Cord

Regularly inspect the power cord for any signs of wear or damage. If you notice any issues, stop using the air fryer and contact Salter customer service.

12. Don't Use Near Flammable Materials

Keep your air fryer away from curtains, paper towels, or any other flammable materials.

13. Unplug When Not in Use

It's a good habit to unplug your air fryer when you're not using it. This saves energy and eliminates any risk of accidental activation.

14. Be Cautious with Wet Batters

Very wet batters can drip during cooking and potentially cause smoking or even fire. If you're using a wet batter, consider freezing the food first or using a liner in the basket.

15. Use Appropriate Accessories

Only use accessories that are specifically designed for use with air fryers. Using the wrong accessories could damage your air fryer or create safety hazards.

Remember, these safety precautions aren't meant to scare you – they're just to ensure you have the best and safest experience with your Salter air fryer. In my years of air frying, I've never had any major issues, and I'm sure you won't either if you follow these guidelines.

Air frying is supposed to be fun and convenient, and with these safety measures in mind, you can focus on the exciting part – creating delicious, healthier meals for you and your loved ones. Happy air frying.

ESSENTIAL TOOLS FOR AIR FRYING

While your Salter air fryer is a powerhouse on its own, having a few key tools on hand can elevate your air frying game. When I first started, I thought all I needed was the air fryer itself. But over time, I've discovered a few essentials that make the process easier, more efficient, and even more enjoyable. Here's my list of must-have tools for air frying:

1. Oil Mister or Spray Bottle

This is probably the tool I use most often with my air fryer. A good oil mister allows you to add just a light coating of oil to your food, which is often all you need for that perfect crispy finish. It's much more efficient than trying to brush oil on, and it helps you use less oil overall.

2. Silicone-Tipped Tongs

A good pair of tongs is essential for safely removing hot food from your air fryer. Look for a pair with silicone tips – they won't scratch the non-stick coating on your basket. I prefer tongs with long handles to keep my hands away from the heat.

3. Heat-Resistant Silicone Spatula

For foods that are a bit more delicate, a silicone spatula can be gentler than tongs. It's also great for stirring or flipping foods mid-cook.

4. Instant-Read Thermometer

This is particularly useful when cooking meats. An instant-read thermometer lets you quickly check if your food has reached a safe internal temperature without losing too much heat from the air fryer.

5. Silicone Baking Cups

These are brilliant for making individual portions of things like egg cups, mini frittatas, or even cupcakes. They're non-stick, reusable, and fit perfectly in most air fryer baskets.

6. Parchment Paper Liners

Pre-cut parchment liners designed for air fryers can be a real time-saver when it comes to clean up. They're especially useful for messy or sticky foods. Just make sure to weigh them down with food so they don't fly up into the heating element.

7. Basting Brush

A silicone basting brush is great for applying marinades or glazes to your food during cooking. It gives you more control than a spray bottle for thicker sauces.

8. Oven Mitts or Heat-Resistant Gloves

These are essential for safely handling the hot basket and drawer. I prefer silicone gloves as they offer good grip and dexterity.

9. Kitchen Scale

While not strictly necessary, a kitchen scale can be very useful for ensuring you're not overloading your air fryer basket. Many recipes specify weights, and getting the right amount of food ensures even cooking.

10. Non-Stick Grill Pan or Baking Dish

These accessories are designed to fit inside your air fryer basket and are great for foods that might stick or foods with sauces. They also make cleanup a breeze.

11. Pastry Brush

This is handy for applying egg wash to pastries or brushing melted butter on foods. I prefer silicone brushes as they're easier to clean and don't shed bristles.

12. Measuring Spoons and Cups

Accurate measurements are key to successful cooking, and air frying is no exception. A good set of measuring spoons and cups will serve you well.

13. Mixing Bowls

A set of various-sized mixing bowls is essential for preparing foods before they go into the air fryer. I like glass bowls as they're microwave-safe, which is handy for melting butter or chocolate.

14. Cooling Rack

A wire cooling rack is great for letting air-fried foods cool without getting soggy. It's particularly useful for things like breaded chicken or fish.

15. Sharp Knife and Cutting Board

While not specific to air frying, a good sharp knife and a sturdy cutting board are essential for prep work. I prefer wooden or bamboo cutting boards as they're gentler on knife edges.

16. Food Storage Containers

If you're batch cooking or have leftovers, a good set of airtight containers is essential. Glass containers are great as they can go from fridge to air fryer for reheating.

Remember, you don't need to rush out and buy all of these at once. Start with the basic☐s tongs, an oil mister, and oven mitts and gradually add to your collection as you explore more recipes and techniques.

I've found that having these tools not only makes air frying easier and more enjoyable but also expands what I can do with my Salter air fryer. From perfectly crispy chips to delicate pastries, having the right tools can take your air frying to the next level.

And don't forget while these tools are helpful, the most important tool is your creativity and willingness to experiment. Some of my best air fryer discoveries have come from trying new things and thinking outside the box. So, grab your tools, fire up that Salter air fryer, and let's get cooking.

MEAL PLANNING AND PREP

One of the best things about your Salter air fryer is how it can streamline your meal planning and prep. When I first got my air fryer, I was mainly using it for one-off meals. But over time, I've discovered how brilliant it is for planning and preparing meals for the whole week. Here's how I approach meal planning and prep with my air fryer:

Remember, meal planning and prep should make your life easier, not add stress. Start small maybe plan just a few days at first and gradually work up to a full week as you get more comfortable.

With a little planning and your trusty Salter air fryer, you'll be amazed at how easy it can be to enjoy healthy, delicious meals all week long. Happy planning and happy air frying.

WEEKLY MEAL PLAN TEMPLATES

Creating a weekly meal plan can seem daunting at first, but with a good template, it becomes much easier. Here is a 6-week meal plan for your adventure. Feel free to adjust these to fit your personal preferences and schedule.

Week 1:

Monday:
- Breakfast: Perfect Bacon Rashers
- Snack: Homemade Crisps
- Lunch: Spinach and Ricotta Stuffed Shells
- Appetizer: Crispy Spring Rolls
- Dinner: Perfect Roast Chicken

Tuesday:
- Breakfast: Fluffy French Toast Sticks
- Snack: Mozzarella Sticks
- Lunch: Veggie Stuffed Peppers
- Appetizer: Mini Quiches
- Dinner: Crispy Skin Salmon

Wednesday:
- Breakfast: Cheesy Egg and Sausage Cups
- Snack: Sweet Potato Fries
- Lunch: Vegetarian Chickpea Curry
- Appetizer: Stuffed Mushrooms
- Dinner: BBQ Pork Chops

Thursday:
- Breakfast: Crispy Hash Browns
- Snack: Crispy Tofu Nuggets
- Lunch: Beef and Broccoli Stir Fry
- Appetizer: Onion Bhajis
- Dinner: Lemon Herb Tilapia

Friday:
- Breakfast: Cinnamon Apple Fritters
- Snack: Garlic Parmesan Potato Wedges
- Lunch: Spinach and Feta Breakfast Tarts
- Appetizer: Homemade Fish Fingers
- Dinner: Buttermilk Fried Chicken

Saturday:
- Breakfast: Breakfast Burrito Rolls
- Snack: Spicy Cauliflower Bites
- Lunch: Parmesan Crusted Cod
- Appetizer: Cheese and Bacon Stuffed Jalapenos
- Dinner: Teriyaki Chicken Skewers

Sunday:
- Breakfast: Yoghurt and Granola Parfait Cups
- Snack: Crispy Chicken Wings
- Lunch: Stuffed Portobello Mushrooms
- Appetizer: Crispy Coconut Shrimp
- Dinner: Garlic Butter Steak Bites

Week 2:
Monday:
- Breakfast: Smoked Salmon and Cream Cheese Bagels
- Snack: Courgette Fritters
- Lunch: Skinny Fish and Chips
- Appetizer: Falafel Bites
- Dinner: Chinese Crispy Duck

Tuesday:
- Breakfast: Vegetable Frittata Squares
- Snack: Crispy Kale Chips
- Lunch: Low-Carb Cauliflower Pizza
- Appetizer: Greek Spanakopita Triangles
- Dinner: German Schnitzel

Wednesday:
- Breakfast: Banana Bread Slices
- Snack: Parmesan Zucchini Fries
- Lunch: Veggie Loaded Frittata
- Appetizer: Mini Beef Empanadas
- Dinner: Indian Tandoori Chicken

Thursday:
- Breakfast: Breakfast Sausage Patties
- Snack: Crispy Onion Rings
- Lunch: Zucchini Nachos
- Appetizer: Mexican Street Corn
- Dinner: Korean Bibimbap Bowl

Friday:
- Breakfast: Blueberry Muffins
- Snack: Maple Roasted Butternut Squash
- Lunch: Turkey Meatballs
- Appetizer: Italian Arancini Balls
- Dinner: Lebanese Kibbeh

Saturday:
- Breakfast: Crispy Potato Rosti
- Snack: Crispy Okra
- Lunch: Eggplant Parmesan
- Appetizer: Japanese Gyoza
- Dinner: Thai Fish Cakes

Sunday:
- Breakfast: Maple Pecan Overnight Oats (reheated)
- Snack: Garlic Mushroom Caps
- Lunch: Crispy Tofu Stir Fry
- Appetizer: Vietnamese Spring Rolls
- Dinner: American Buffalo Chicken Tenders

Week 3:

Monday:
- Breakfast: Perfect Bacon Rashers
- Snack: Sesame Asparagus Spears
- Lunch: Buffalo Cauliflower Bites
- Appetizer: Crispy Vegetable Samosas
- Dinner: BBQ Pulled Pork (reheated)

Tuesday:
- Breakfast: Fluffy French Toast Sticks
- Snack: Crispy Eggplant Rounds
- Lunch: Portobello Mushroom Pizzas
- Appetizer: Bacon-Wrapped Scallops
- Dinner: Honey Garlic Glazed Meatballs

Wednesday:
- Breakfast: Cheesy Egg and Sausage Cups
- Snack: Homemade Chicken Nuggets
- Lunch: Baked Falafel
- Appetizer: Mini Quiche Lorraine
- Dinner: Crispy Coconut Chicken

Thursday:
- Breakfast: Crispy Hash Browns
- Snack: Mini Pizzas
- Lunch: Veggie Chips Medley
- Appetizer: Spinach and Artichoke Dip Cups
- Dinner: Sesame Crusted Tuna Steaks

Friday:
- Breakfast: Cinnamon Apple Fritters
- Snack: Crispy Fish Fingers

- Lunch: Stuffed Bell Pepper Boats
- Appetizer: Crispy Coconut Prawns
- Dinner: Perfect Roast Chicken

Saturday:
- Breakfast: Breakfast Burrito Rolls
- Snack: Mac and Cheese Bites
- Lunch: Homemade Fish Fingers
- Appetizer: Buffalo Chicken Dip Wonton Cups
- Dinner: Crispy Skin Salmon

Sunday:
- Breakfast: Yoghurt and Granola Parfait Cups
- Snack: Sweet Potato Tots
- Lunch: Crispy Chicken Tenders
- Appetizer: Jalapeno Popper Bites
- Dinner: BBQ Pork Chops

Week 4:

Monday:
- Breakfast: Smoked Salmon and Cream Cheese Bagels
- Snack: Cheesy Broccoli Fritters
- Lunch: Veggie Stuffed Peppers
- Appetizer: Miniature Beef Wellingtons
- Dinner: Vegetarian Chickpea Curry

Tuesday:
- Breakfast: Vegetable Frittata Squares
- Snack: Crispy Corn Dogs
- Lunch: Beef and Broccoli Stir Fry
- Appetizer: Garlic Parmesan Chicken Wings
- Dinner: Lemon Herb Tilapia

Wednesday:
- Breakfast: Banana Bread Slices
- Snack: Apple Cinnamon Chips
- Lunch: Spinach and Feta Breakfast Tarts
- Appetizer: Stuffed Mushroom Caps

- Dinner: Buttermilk Fried Chicken

Thursday:
- Breakfast: Breakfast Sausage Patties
- Snack: Carrot Fries
- Lunch: Parmesan Crusted Cod
- Appetizer: Crispy Bruschetta Bites
- Dinner: Teriyaki Chicken Skewers

Friday:
- Breakfast: Blueberry Muffins
- Snack: Crispy Tofu Fingers
- Lunch: Stuffed Portobello Mushrooms
- Appetizer: Bacon-wrapped asparagus Bundles
- Dinner: Garlic Butter Steak Bites

Saturday:
- Breakfast: Crispy Potato Rosti
- Snack: Zucchini Pizza Bites
- Lunch: Skinny Fish and Chips
- Appetizer: Mini Crab Cakes
- Dinner: Chinese Crispy Duck

Sunday:
- Breakfast: Maple Pecan Overnight Oats (reheated)
- Snack: Peanut Butter Banana Roll-Ups
- Lunch: Low-Carb Cauliflower Pizza
- Appetizer: Brie and Cranberry Parcels
- Dinner: German Schnitzel

Week 5:

Monday:
- Breakfast: Perfect Bacon Rashers
- Snack: Crispy Chicken Sliders
- Lunch: Veggie Loaded Frittata
- Appetizer: Spinach and Feta Spanakopita
- Dinner: Indian Tandoori Chicken

Tuesday:
- Breakfast: Fluffy French Toast Sticks
- Snack: Cauliflower Popcorn
- Lunch: Zucchini Nachos
- Appetizer: BBQ Pulled Pork Sliders
- Dinner: Korean Bibimbap Bowl

Wednesday:
- Breakfast: Cheesy Egg and Sausage Cups
- Snack: Cinnamon Sugar Donut Holes
- Lunch: Turkey Meatballs
- Appetizer: Apple Fritters
- Dinner: Lebanese Kibbeh

Thursday:
- Breakfast: Crispy Hash Browns
- Snack: Chocolate Lava Cakes
- Lunch: Eggplant Parmesan
- Appetizer: Cinnamon Sugar Churros
- Dinner: Thai Fish Cakes

Friday:
- Breakfast: Cinnamon Apple Fritters
- Snack: Berry Crumble
- Lunch: Crispy Tofu Stir Fry
- Appetizer: Banana Bread
- Dinner: American Buffalo Chicken Tenders

Saturday:
- Breakfast: Breakfast Burrito Rolls
- Snack: Mini Cheesecakes
- Lunch: Buffalo Cauliflower Bites
- Appetizer: Peach Cobbler
- Dinner: BBQ Pulled Pork (reheated)

Sunday:
- Breakfast: Yoghurt and Granola Parfait Cups
- Snack: Peanut Butter Cookies
- Lunch: Portobello Mushroom Pizzas
- Appetizer: Crispy Cinnamon Rolls
- Dinner: Honey Garlic Glazed Meatballs

Week 6:

Monday:
- Breakfast: Smoked Salmon and Cream Cheese Bagels
- Snack: Baked Apples
- Lunch: Baked Falafel
- Appetizer: Chocolate Chip Cookie Cups
- Dinner: Crispy Coconut Chicken

Tuesday:
- Breakfast: Vegetable Frittata Squares
- Snack: Blueberry Muffins
- Lunch: Veggie Chips Medley
- Appetizer: Crispy Fruit Spring Rolls
- Dinner: Sesame Crusted Tuna Steaks

Wednesday:
- Breakfast: Banana Bread Slices
- Snack: Lemon Drizzle Cake Slices
- Lunch: Stuffed Bell Pepper Boats
- Appetizer: Strawberry Shortcake Stacks
- Dinner: Perfect Roast Chicken

Thursday:
- Breakfast: Breakfast Sausage Patties
- Snack: Garlic Aioli with vegetable sticks
- Lunch: Crispy Chicken Tenders
- Appetizer: Spicy Sriracha Mayo with fries
- Dinner: Crispy Skin Salmon

Friday:
- Breakfast: Blueberry Muffins
- Snack: Homemade Tomato Ketchup with nuggets
- Lunch: Veggie Stuffed Peppers
- Appetizer: Honey Mustard Dip with chicken strips
- Dinner: BBQ Pork Chops

Saturday:
- Breakfast: Crispy Potato Rosti
- Snack: Sweet Chili Sauce with spring rolls
- Lunch: Beef and Broccoli Stir Fry
- Appetizer: Tzatziki Sauce with falafel
- Dinner: Vegetarian Chickpea Curry

Sunday:
- Breakfast: Maple Pecan Overnight Oats (reheated)
- Snack: Barbecue Sauce with chicken wings
- Lunch: Spinach and Feta Breakfast Tarts
- Appetizer: Ranch Dressing with vegetable sticks
- Dinner: Lemon Herb Tilapia

This meal plan provides variety throughout the six weeks, remember to adjust portion sizes and ingredients according to your dietary needs and preferences.

CHAPTER 1: BREAKFAST DELIGHTS

Perfect Bacon Rashers

Prep: 5 mins Cook: 10 mins Serves: 4

Ingredients:

US: 8 rashers of bacon, 1 tablespoon maple syrup (optional)

UK: 8 rashers of bacon, 1 tablespoon maple syrup (optional)

Instructions:

1. Preheat your Salter Air Fryer to 200°C (392°F) for about 3 minutes.
2. Place the bacon rashers in a single layer in the air fryer basket.
3. Cook for 8-10 minutes, turning halfway through, until crispy and golden.
4. If you like a sweet touch, brush the bacon with maple syrup during the last 2 minutes of cooking.
5. Remove from the air fryer and let them drain on a paper towel before serving.

Nutritional Info: Calories: 150 Fat: 12g Carbs: 1g Protein: 10g

Fluffy French Toast Sticks

Prep: 10 mins Cook: 8 mins Serves: 4

Ingredients:

US: 4 slices of bread, 2 large eggs, 60ml milk, 1 teaspoon vanilla extract, 1 teaspoon cinnamon, 30g sugar, 30ml maple syrup (for serving)

UK: 4 slices of bread, 2 large eggs, 60ml milk, 1 teaspoon vanilla extract, 1 teaspoon cinnamon, 30g sugar, 30ml maple syrup (for serving)

Instructions:

1. Preheat your Salter Air Fryer to 180°C (356°F).
2. Cut each slice of bread into three sticks.
3. In a bowl, whisk together the eggs, milk, vanilla extract, and cinnamon.
4. Dip the breadsticks into the egg mixture, ensuring they are fully coated.
5. Place the sticks in the air fryer basket, making sure they are not touching.
6. Cook for 8 minutes, turning halfway through, until golden brown.
7. Sprinkle with sugar and serve with maple syrup.

Nutritional Info: Calories: 200 Fat: 6g Carbs: 28g Protein: 7g

Ceesy Egg and Sausage Cups

Prep: 10 mins Cook: 15 mins Serves: 4

Ingredients:

US: 4 large eggs, 120g cooked sausage (crumbled), 60g shredded cheddar cheese, 2 tablespoons chopped chives, salt, pepper

UK: 4 large eggs, 120g cooked sausage (crumbled), 60g shredded cheddar cheese, 2 tablespoons chopped chives, salt, pepper

Instructions:

1. Preheat your Salter Air Fryer to 180°C (356°F).
2. In a bowl, beat the eggs and season with salt and pepper.
3. Add the crumbled sausage, cheese, and chives to the eggs and mix well.
4. Divide the mixture evenly into silicone muffin cups.
5. Place the cups in the air fryer basket and cook for 12-15 minutes, until the eggs are set and the tops are slightly golden.
6. Let them cool slightly before removing from the cups and serving.

Nutritional Info: Calories: 250 Fat: 20g Carbs: 2g Protein: 18g

Crispy Hash Browns

Prep: 10 mins Cook: 20 mins Serves: 4

Ingredients:

US: 500g potatoes (peeled and grated), 1 small onion (grated), 1 egg, 2 tablespoons flour, salt, pepper, 2 tablespoons olive oil

UK: 500g potatoes (peeled and grated), 1 small onion (grated), 1 egg, 2 tablespoons flour, salt, pepper, 2 tablespoons olive oil

Instructions:

1. Preheat your Salter Air Fryer to 200°C (392°F).
2. Squeeze out any excess moisture from the grated potatoes and onion.
3. In a bowl, mix the potatoes, onion, egg, flour, salt, and pepper until well combined.
4. Form the mixture into small patties.
5. Brush the patties with olive oil on both sides.
6. Place the patties in the air fryer basket in a single layer.
7. Cook for 15-20 minutes, flipping halfway through, until golden and crispy.

Nutritional Info: Calories: 180 Fat: 7g Carbs: 25g Protein: 4g

Cinnamon Apple Fritters

Prep: 10 mins Cook: 10 mins Serves: 4

Ingredients:

US: 2 large apples (peeled, cored, and diced), 100g flour, 2 tablespoons sugar, 1 teaspoon cinnamon, 1 teaspoon baking powder, 1/4 teaspoon salt, 1 large egg, 60ml milk, 2 tablespoons butter (melted), 30g powdered sugar (for dusting)

UK: 2 large apples (peeled, cored, and diced), 100g flour, 2 tablespoons sugar, 1 teaspoon cinnamon, 1 teaspoon baking powder, 1/4 teaspoon salt, 1 large egg, 60ml milk, 2 tablespoons butter (melted), 30g powdered sugar (for dusting)

Instructions:

1. Preheat your Salter Air Fryer to 180°C (356°F).
2. In a bowl, whisk together the flour, sugar, cinnamon, baking powder, and salt.
3. In another bowl, beat the egg, then add the milk and melted butter.
4. Add the wet ingredients to the dry ingredients and stir until just combined.
5. Fold in the diced apples.
6. Drop spoonfuls of the batter into the air fryer basket lined with parchment paper.
7. Cook for 8-10 minutes, until golden brown.
8. Dust with powdered sugar before serving.

Nutritional Info: Calories: 220 Fat: 7g Carbs: 36g Protein: 4g

Breakfast Burrito Rolls

Prep: 15 mins Cook: 10 mins Serves: 4

Ingredients:

US: 4 large tortillas, 4 large eggs, 120g cooked sausage (crumbled), 100g shredded cheddar cheese, 1 small bell pepper (diced), 1 small onion (diced), salt, pepper, 1 tablespoon olive oil

UK: 4 large tortillas, 4 large eggs, 120g cooked sausage (crumbled), 100g shredded cheddar cheese, 1 small bell pepper (diced), 1 small onion (diced), salt, pepper, 1 tablespoon olive oil

Instructions:

1. Preheat your Salter Air Fryer to 180°C (356°F).
2. In a pan, heat the olive oil over medium heat and sauté the bell pepper and onion until soft.
3. Add the crumbled sausage and cook until heated through.
4. In a bowl, beat the eggs and season with salt and pepper.
5. Pour the eggs into the pan with the sausage and vegetables, stirring until scrambled and cooked through.
6. Divide the egg mixture among the tortillas and sprinkle with cheese.
7. Roll up the tortillas and place them seam-side down in the air fryer basket.
8. Cook for 5-7 minutes, until the tortillas are crispy and the cheese is melted.

Nutritional Info: Calories: 300 Fat: 15g Carbs: 25g Protein: 16g

Yoghurt and Granola Parfait Cups

Prep: 10 mins Cook: 0 mins Serves: 4

Ingredients:

US: 500g Greek yoghurt, 200g granola, 100g mixed berries, 2 tablespoons honey
UK: 500g Greek yoghurt, 200g granola, 100g mixed berries, 2 tablespoons honey

Instructions:

1. In each serving cup, layer 125g of Greek yoghurt.
2. Add 50g of granola on top of the yoghurt.
3. Layer with 25g of mixed berries.
4. Drizzle with honey.
5. Serve immediately or refrigerate for later.

Nutritional Info: Calories: 250 Fat: 8g Carbs: 34g Protein: 10g

Smoked Salmon and Cream Cheese Bagels

Prep: 10 mins Cook: 0 mins Serves: 4

Ingredients:

US: 4 bagels, 200g smoked salmon, 200g cream cheese, 1 small red onion (thinly sliced), capers (optional), fresh dill (for garnish), lemon wedges
UK: 4 bagels, 200g smoked salmon, 200g cream cheese, 1 small red onion (thinly sliced), capers (optional), fresh dill (for garnish), lemon wedges

Instructions:

1. Slice the bagels in half and toast them in your Salter Air Fryer at 180°C (356°F) for 3-4 minutes until golden.
2. Spread cream cheese on each half.
3. Layer with smoked salmon.
4. Top with sliced red onion and capers if desired.
5. Garnish with fresh dill and serve with lemon wedges.

Nutritional Info: Calories: 300 Fat: 15g Carbs: 30g Protein: 12g

Vegetable Frittata Squares

Prep: 10 mins Cook: 15 mins Serves: 4

Ingredients:

US: 6 large eggs, 100g mixed vegetables (e.g., bell peppers, spinach, mushrooms), 50g shredded cheese, 2 tablespoons milk, salt, pepper, 1 tablespoon olive oil

UK: 6 large eggs, 100g mixed vegetables (e.g., bell peppers, spinach, mushrooms), 50g shredded cheese, 2 tablespoons milk, salt, pepper, 1 tablespoon olive oil

Instructions:

1. Preheat your Salter Air Fryer to 180°C (356°F).
2. In a bowl, beat the eggs with milk, salt, and pepper.
3. Heat olive oil in a pan and sauté the vegetables until soft.
4. Add the vegetables and cheese to the egg mixture.
5. Pour the mixture into a greased baking dish that fits your air fryer.
6. Cook for 12-15 minutes, until the eggs are set and slightly golden.
7. Let cool slightly before cutting into squares and serving.

Nutritional Info: Calories: 220 Fat: 15g Carbs: 4g Protein: 16g

Banana Bread Slices

Prep: 15 mins Cook: 25 mins Serves: 8

Ingredients:

US: 3 ripe bananas (mashed), 200g flour, 150g sugar, 1 teaspoon baking soda, 1/2 teaspoon salt, 1 teaspoon vanilla extract, 1 large egg, 60ml vegetable oil

UK: 3 ripe bananas (mashed), 200g flour, 150g sugar, 1 teaspoon baking soda, 1/2 teaspoon salt, 1 teaspoon vanilla extract, 1 large egg, 60ml vegetable oil

Instructions:

1. Preheat your Salter Air Fryer to 160°C (320°F).
2. In a bowl, mix the mashed bananas, sugar, egg, and vanilla extract.
3. Add the flour, baking soda, and salt, and mix until just combined.
4. Stir in the vegetable oil.
5. Pour the batter into a greased baking dish that fits your air fryer.
6. Cook for 20-25 minutes, until a toothpick inserted into the centre comes out clean.
7. Let cool before slicing and serving.

Nutritional Info: Calories: 250 Fat: 8g Carbs: 40g Protein: 3g

Breakfast Sausage Patties

Prep: 10 mins Cook: 10 mins Serves: 4

Ingredients:

US: 500g ground pork, 1 teaspoon sage, 1 teaspoon thyme, 1 teaspoon paprika, 1/2 teaspoon garlic powder, 1/2 teaspoon onion powder, salt, pepper

UK: 500g ground pork, 1 teaspoon sage, 1 teaspoon thyme, 1 teaspoon paprika, 1/2 teaspoon garlic powder, 1/2 teaspoon onion powder, salt, pepper

Instructions:

1. In a bowl, mix the ground pork with all the spices until well combined.
2. Form the mixture into small patties.
3. Preheat your Salter Air Fryer to 200°C (392°F).
4. Place the patties in the air fryer basket in a single layer.
5. Cook for 8-10 minutes, flipping halfway through, until fully cooked and browned.

Nutritional Info: Calories: 200 Fat: 15g Carbs: 1g Protein: 15g

Spinach and Feta Breakfast Tarts

Prep: 15 mins Cook: 12 mins Serves: 4

Ingredients:

US: 1 sheet puff pastry, 100g fresh spinach (chopped), 100g feta cheese (crumbled), 2 large eggs, 2 tablespoons milk, salt, pepper

UK: 1 sheet puff pastry, 100g fresh spinach (chopped), 100g feta cheese (crumbled), 2 large eggs, 2 tablespoons milk, salt, pepper

Instructions:

1. Preheat your Salter Air Fryer to 180°C (356°F).
2. Cut the puff pastry into 4 squares and place them in tart tins or on a lined air fryer basket.
3. In a bowl, beat the eggs with milk, salt, and pepper.
4. Evenly distribute the chopped spinach and feta cheese among the pastry squares.
5. Pour the egg mixture over the spinach and feta.
6. Cook for 10-12 minutes, until the pastry is golden and the egg is set.

Nutritional Info: Calories: 300 Fat: 20g Carbs: 20g Protein: 8g

Blueberry Muffins

Prep: 15 mins Cook: 15 mins Serves: 6

Ingredients:

US: 200g flour, 100g sugar, 2 teaspoons baking powder, 1/2 teaspoon salt, 1 large egg, 120ml milk, 60ml vegetable oil, 150g blueberries

UK: 200g flour, 100g sugar, 2 teaspoons baking powder, 1/2 teaspoon salt, 1 large egg, 120ml milk, 60ml vegetable oil, 150g blueberries

Instructions:

1. Preheat your Salter Air Fryer to 180°C (356°F).
2. In a bowl, mix the flour, sugar, baking powder, and salt.
3. In another bowl, beat the egg, then add the milk and vegetable oil.
4. Add the wet ingredients to the dry ingredients and stir until just combined.
5. Gently fold in the blueberries.
6. Divide the batter into silicone muffin cups.
7. Place the cups in the air fryer basket and cook for 12-15 minutes, until a toothpick inserted into the centre comes out clean.

Nutritional Info: Calories: 200 Fat: 8g Carbs: 30g Protein: 3g

Crispy Potato Rosti

Prep: 10 mins Cook: 20 mins Serves: 4

Ingredients:

US: 500g potatoes (peeled and grated), 1 small onion (grated), 1 egg, 2 tablespoons flour, salt, pepper, 2 tablespoons olive oil

UK: 500g potatoes (peeled and grated), 1 small onion (grated), 1 egg, 2 tablespoons flour, salt, pepper, 2 tablespoons olive oil

Instructions:

1. Preheat your Salter Air Fryer to 200°C (392°F).
2. Squeeze out any excess moisture from the grated potatoes and onion.
3. In a bowl, mix the potatoes, onion, egg, flour, salt, and pepper until well combined.
4. Form the mixture into small patties.
5. Brush the patties with olive oil on both sides.
6. Place the patties in the air fryer basket in a single layer.
7. Cook for 15-20 minutes, flipping halfway through, until golden and crispy.

Nutritional Info: Calories: 180 Fat: 7g Carbs: 25g Protein: 4g

Maple Pecan Overnight Oats (for reheating)

Prep: 10 mins Cook: 0 mins Serves: 4

Ingredients:

US: 200g rolled oats, 500ml milk, 2 tablespoons maple syrup, 50g pecans (chopped), 1 teaspoon vanilla extract, 1/2 teaspoon cinnamon

UK: 200g rolled oats, 500ml milk, 2 tablespoons maple syrup, 50g pecans (chopped), 1 teaspoon vanilla extract, 1/2 teaspoon cinnamon

Instructions:

1. In a bowl, mix the oats, milk, maple syrup, pecans, vanilla extract, and cinnamon.
2. Divide the mixture into 4 jars or containers.
3. Cover and refrigerate overnight.
4. To reheat, place a portion in a microwave-safe bowl and heat on high for 1-2 minutes, or until warmed through. Alternatively, heat in the Salter Air Fryer at 160°C (320°F) for 5-7 minutes.

Nutritional Info: Calories: 250 Fat: 10g Carbs: 36g Protein: 6g

CHAPTER 2: SCRUMPTIOUS SNACKS AND STARTERS

Crispy Chicken Wings

Prep: 10 mins Cook: 25 mins Serves: 4

Ingredients:

US: 1kg chicken wings, 2 tablespoons olive oil, 1 teaspoon paprika, 1 teaspoon garlic powder, 1 teaspoon onion powder, 1 teaspoon salt, 1/2 teaspoon black pepper

UK: 1kg chicken wings, 2 tablespoons olive oil, 1 teaspoon paprika, 1 teaspoon garlic powder, 1 teaspoon onion powder, 1 teaspoon salt, 1/2 teaspoon black pepper

Instructions:

1. Preheat your Salter Air Fryer to 200°C (392°F).
2. In a large bowl, toss the chicken wings with olive oil, paprika, garlic powder, onion powder, salt, and black pepper until well coated.
3. Arrange the wings in a single layer in the air fryer basket.
4. Cook for 25 minutes, turning halfway through, until crispy and golden.
5. Serve hot with your favourite dipping sauce.

Nutritional Info: Calories: 300 Fat: 20g Carbs: 1g Protein: 25g

Mozzarella Sticks

Prep: 15 mins Cook: 10 mins Serves: 4

Ingredients:

US: 200g mozzarella cheese (cut into sticks), 50g flour, 2 large eggs (beaten), 100g breadcrumbs, 1 teaspoon dried oregano, 1 teaspoon dried basil, 1/2 teaspoon garlic powder, salt, pepper, olive oil spray

UK: 200g mozzarella cheese (cut into sticks), 50g flour, 2 large eggs (beaten), 100g breadcrumbs, 1 teaspoon dried oregano, 1 teaspoon dried basil, 1/2 teaspoon garlic powder, salt, pepper, olive oil spray

Instructions:

1. Preheat your Salter Air Fryer to 180°C (356°F).
2. Set up a breading station with flour, beaten eggs, and breadcrumbs mixed with oregano, basil, garlic powder, salt, and pepper.
3. Dip each mozzarella sticks in flour, then egg, and finally coat with breadcrumbs.
4. Arrange the sticks in the air fryer basket and spray lightly with olive oil.
5. Cook for 8-10 minutes, turning halfway through, until golden and crispy.

6. Serve with marinara sauce for dipping.

Nutritional Info: Calories: 250 Fat: 15g Carbs: 15g Protein: 12g

Homemade Crisps

Prep: 10 mins Cook: 20 mins Serves: 4

Ingredients:

US: 500g potatoes (thinly sliced), 2 tablespoons olive oil, salt, pepper

UK: 500g potatoes (thinly sliced), 2 tablespoons olive oil, salt, pepper

Instructions:

1. Preheat your Salter Air Fryer to 180°C (356°F).
2. Toss the thinly sliced potatoes in olive oil, salt, and pepper.
3. Arrange the potato slices in a single layer in the air fryer basket.
4. Cook for 15-20 minutes, shaking the basket occasionally, until crispy and golden brown.
5. Serve immediately as a crunchy snack.

Nutritional Info: Calories: 150 Fat: 7g Carbs: 20g Protein: 2g

Garlic Parmesan Potato Wedges

Prep: 10 mins Cook: 25 mins Serves: 4

Ingredients:

US: 500g potatoes (cut into wedges), 2 tablespoons olive oil, 3 tablespoons grated Parmesan cheese, 1 teaspoon garlic powder, 1 teaspoon dried parsley, salt, pepper

UK: 500g potatoes (cut into wedges), 2 tablespoons olive oil, 3 tablespoons grated Parmesan cheese, 1 teaspoon garlic powder, 1 teaspoon dried parsley, salt, pepper

Instructions:

1. Preheat your Salter Air Fryer to 200°C (392°F).
2. In a bowl, toss the potato wedges with olive oil, Parmesan cheese, garlic powder, dried parsley, salt, and pepper.
3. Arrange the wedges in a single layer in the air fryer basket.
4. Cook for 20-25 minutes, turning halfway through, until golden and crispy.
5. Serve hot with your favourite dipping sauce.

Nutritional Info: Calories: 200 Fat: 8g Carbs: 30g Protein: 4g

Spicy Cauliflower Bites

Prep: 10 mins Cook: 15 mins Serves: 4

Ingredients:

US: 1 large cauliflower (cut into florets), 2 tablespoons olive oil, 1 teaspoon smoked paprika, 1 teaspoon garlic powder, 1/2 teaspoon cayenne pepper, salt, pepper

UK: 1 large cauliflower (cut into florets), 2 tablespoons olive oil, 1 teaspoon smoked paprika, 1 teaspoon garlic powder, 1/2 teaspoon cayenne pepper, salt, pepper

Instructions:

1. Preheat your Salter Air Fryer to 200°C (392°F).
2. In a bowl, toss the cauliflower florets with olive oil, smoked paprika, garlic powder, cayenne pepper, salt, and pepper.
3. Arrange the cauliflower in a single layer in the air fryer basket.
4. Cook for 12-15 minutes, shaking the basket halfway through, until tender and crispy.
5. Serve with a cooling dip like ranch or blue cheese.

Nutritional Info: Calories: 100 Fat: 7g Carbs: 8g Protein: 3g

Mini Quiches

Prep: 15 mins Cook: 15 mins Serves: 4

Ingredients:

US: 4 large eggs, 120ml milk, 50g grated cheese, 50g cooked ham (diced), 1 small bell pepper (diced), salt, pepper, 1 tablespoon olive oil

UK: 4 large eggs, 120ml milk, 50g grated cheese, 50g cooked ham (diced), 1 small bell pepper (diced), salt, pepper, 1 tablespoon olive oil

Instructions:

1. Preheat your Salter Air Fryer to 180°C (356°F).
2. In a bowl, beat the eggs with milk, salt, and pepper.
3. Stir in the grated cheese, diced ham, and bell pepper.
4. Grease silicone muffin cups with olive oil and divide the mixture evenly among them.
5. Place the muffin cups in the air fryer basket and cook for 12-15 minutes, until the quiches are set and slightly golden.
6. Let cool slightly before serving.

Nutritional Info: Calories: 200 Fat: 15g Carbs: 2g Protein: 12g

Crispy Spring Rolls

Prep: 20 mins Cook: 15 mins Serves: 4

Ingredients:

US: 8 spring roll wrappers, 200g mixed vegetables (shredded), 100g cooked chicken (shredded), 2 tablespoons soy sauce, 1 teaspoon sesame oil, 1 teaspoon grated ginger, olive oil spray

UK: 8 spring roll wrappers, 200g mixed vegetables (shredded), 100g cooked chicken (shredded), 2 tablespoons soy sauce, 1 teaspoon sesame oil, 1 teaspoon grated ginger, olive oil spray

Instructions:

1. Preheat your Salter Air Fryer to 200°C (392°F).
2. In a bowl, combine the mixed vegetables, cooked chicken, soy sauce, sesame oil, and grated ginger.
3. Place a spoonful of the mixture on each spring roll wrapper and roll tightly, sealing the edges with water.
4. Arrange the spring rolls in the air fryer basket and spray lightly with olive oil.
5. Cook for 12-15 minutes, turning halfway through, until golden and crispy.
6. Serve with sweet chilli sauce for dipping.

Nutritional Info: Calories: 150 Fat: 5g Carbs: 20g Protein: 8g

Stuffed Mushrooms

Prep: 10 mins Cook: 12 mins Serves: 4

Ingredients:

US: 12 large mushrooms (stems removed), 100g cream cheese, 50g grated Parmesan cheese, 2 tablespoons chopped fresh parsley, 1 clove garlic (minced), salt, pepper, olive oil spray

UK: 12 large mushrooms (stems removed), 100g cream cheese, 50g grated Parmesan cheese, 2 tablespoons chopped fresh parsley, 1 clove garlic (minced), salt, pepper, olive oil spray

Instructions:

1. Preheat your Salter Air Fryer to 180°C (356°F).
2. In a bowl, mix the cream cheese, grated Parmesan, chopped parsley, minced garlic, salt, and pepper.
3. Stuff each mushroom with the cream cheese mixture.
4. Arrange the stuffed mushrooms in the air fryer basket and spray lightly with olive oil.
5. Cook for 10-12 minutes, until the mushrooms are tender and the filling is golden.
6. Serve warm as a delicious appetiser.

Nutritional Info: Calories: 100 Fat: 8g Carbs: 2g Protein: 4g

Onion Bhajis

Prep: 15 mins Cook: 10 mins Serves: 4

Ingredients:

US: 2 large onions (thinly sliced), 100g gram flour (chickpea flour), 1 teaspoon cumin seeds, 1 teaspoon coriander seeds, 1 teaspoon turmeric, 1 teaspoon chilli powder, 1/2 teaspoon baking powder, salt, water, olive oil spray

UK: 2 large onions (thinly sliced), 100g gram flour (chickpea flour), 1 teaspoon cumin seeds, 1 teaspoon coriander seeds, 1 teaspoon turmeric, 1 teaspoon chilli powder, 1/2 teaspoon baking powder, salt, water, olive oil spray

Instructions:

1. Preheat your Salter Air Fryer to 180°C (356°F).
2. In a bowl, combine the sliced onions with gram flour, cumin seeds, coriander seeds, turmeric, chilli powder, baking powder, and salt.
3. Add enough water to form a thick batter that coats the onions.
4. Drop spoonfuls of the mixture into the air fryer basket and spray lightly with olive oil.
5. Cook for 8-10 minutes, until golden and crispy.
6. Serve with chutney or yoghurt dip.

Nutritional Info: Calories: 150 Fat: 5g Carbs: 20g Protein: 4g

Homemade Fish Fingers

Prep: 15 mins Cook: 10 mins Serves: 4

Ingredients:

US: 400g white fish fillets (cut into strips), 50g flour, 2 large eggs (beaten), 100g breadcrumbs, 1 teaspoon paprika, 1/2 teaspoon garlic powder, salt, pepper, olive oil spray

UK: 400g white fish fillets (cut into strips), 50g flour, 2 large eggs (beaten), 100g breadcrumbs, 1 teaspoon paprika, 1/2 teaspoon garlic powder, salt, pepper, olive oil spray

Instructions:

1. Preheat your Salter Air Fryer to 200°C (392°F).
2. Set up a breading station with flour, beaten eggs, and breadcrumbs mixed with paprika, garlic powder, salt, and pepper.
3. Dip each fish strip in flour, then egg, and finally coat with breadcrumbs.
4. Arrange the fish fingers in the air fryer basket and spray lightly with olive oil.
5. Cook for 8-10 minutes, turning halfway through, until golden and crispy.
6. Serve with tartar sauce and lemon wedges.

Nutritional Info: Calories: 200 Fat: 8g Carbs: 20g Protein: 15g

Courgette Fritters

Prep: 10 mins Cook: 15 mins Serves: 4

Ingredients:

US: 2 medium courgettes (grated), 1 small onion (grated), 2 large eggs, 50g flour, 1 teaspoon baking powder, salt, pepper, olive oil spray

UK: 2 medium courgettes (grated), 1 small onion (grated), 2 large eggs, 50g flour, 1 teaspoon baking powder, salt, pepper, olive oil spray

Instructions:

1. Preheat your Salter Air Fryer to 180°C (356°F).
2. Squeeze out any excess moisture from the grated courgettes and onion.
3. In a bowl, mix the courgettes, onion, eggs, flour, baking powder, salt, and pepper until well combined.
4. Form the mixture into small patties.
5. Arrange the fritters in the air fryer basket and spray lightly with olive oil.
6. Cook for 12-15 minutes, turning halfway through, until golden and crispy.
7. Serve with a dollop of Greek yoghurt or sour cream.

Nutritional Info: Calories: 120 Fat: 5g Carbs: 12g Protein: 4g

Crispy Tofu Nuggets

Prep: 10 mins Cook: 15 mins Serves: 4

Ingredients:

US: 400g firm tofu (cut into cubes), 2 tablespoons soy sauce, 1 tablespoon olive oil, 50g cornflour, 1 teaspoon garlic powder, 1 teaspoon paprika, salt, pepper, olive oil spray

UK: 400g firm tofu (cut into cubes), 2 tablespoons soy sauce, 1 tablespoon olive oil, 50g cornflour, 1 teaspoon garlic powder, 1 teaspoon paprika, salt, pepper, olive oil spray

Instructions:

1. Preheat your Salter Air Fryer to 200°C (392°F).
2. In a bowl, toss the tofu cubes with soy sauce and olive oil.
3. In another bowl, mix the cornflour, garlic powder, paprika, salt, and pepper.
4. Coat the tofu cubes in the cornflour mixture.
5. Arrange the tofu in a single layer in the air fryer basket and spray lightly with olive oil.
6. Cook for 12-15 minutes, shaking the basket halfway through, until crispy and golden.

7. Serve with your favourite dipping sauce.

Nutritional Info: Calories: 150 Fat: 8g Carbs: 10g Protein: 10g

Sweet Potato Fries

Prep: 10 mins Cook: 20 mins Serves: 4

Ingredients:

US: 500g sweet potatoes (cut into fries), 2 tablespoons olive oil, 1 teaspoon smoked paprika, 1/2 teaspoon garlic powder, salt, pepper

UK: 500g sweet potatoes (cut into fries), 2 tablespoons olive oil, 1 teaspoon smoked paprika, 1/2 teaspoon garlic powder, salt, pepper

Instructions:

1. Preheat your Salter Air Fryer to 200°C (392°F).
2. In a bowl, toss the sweet potato fries with olive oil, smoked paprika, garlic powder, salt, and pepper.
3. Arrange the fries in a single layer in the air fryer basket.
4. Cook for 15-20 minutes, shaking the basket occasionally, until crispy and golden.
5. Serve immediately with your favourite dipping sauce.

Nutritional Info: Calories: 180 Fat: 7g Carbs: 28g Protein: 2g

Cheese and Bacon Stuffed Jalapenos

Prep: 10 mins Cook: 12 mins Serves: 4

Ingredients:

US: 12 jalapenos (halved and seeded), 100g cream cheese, 50g grated cheddar cheese, 50g cooked bacon (crumbled), 1 teaspoon garlic powder, salt, pepper, olive oil spray

UK: 12 jalapenos (halved and seeded), 100g cream cheese, 50g grated cheddar cheese, 50g cooked bacon (crumbled), 1 teaspoon garlic powder, salt, pepper, olive oil spray

Instructions:

1. Preheat your Salter Air Fryer to 180°C (356°F).
2. In a bowl, mix the cream cheese, grated cheddar, crumbled bacon, garlic powder, salt, and pepper.
3. Stuff each jalapeno half with the cheese mixture.
4. Arrange the stuffed jalapenos in the air fryer basket and spray lightly with olive oil.
5. Cook for 10-12 minutes, until the jalapenos are tender and the filling is golden.
6. Serve warm as a spicy appetiser.

Nutritional Info: Calories: 150 Fat: 12g Carbs: 4g Protein: 6g

Crispy Coconut Shrimp

Prep: 15 mins Cook: 10 mins Serves: 4

Ingredients:

US: 400g large shrimp (peeled and deveined), 50g flour, 2 large eggs (beaten), 100g shredded coconut, 50g breadcrumbs, 1 teaspoon paprika, salt, pepper, olive oil spray

UK: 400g large shrimp (peeled and deveined), 50g flour, 2 large eggs (beaten), 100g shredded coconut, 50g breadcrumbs, 1 teaspoon paprika, salt, pepper, olive oil spray

Instructions:

1. Preheat your Salter Air Fryer to 200°C (392°F).
2. Set up a breading station with flour, beaten eggs, and a mixture of shredded coconut, breadcrumbs, paprika, salt, and pepper.
3. Dip each shrimp in flour, then egg, and finally coat with the coconut mixture.
4. Arrange the shrimp in the air fryer basket and spray lightly with olive oil.
5. Cook for 8-10 minutes, turning halfway through, until golden and crispy.
6. Serve with a sweet chilli dipping sauce.

Nutritional Info: Calories: 220 Fat: 10g Carbs: 20g Protein: 12g

CHAPTER 3: MOUTHWATERING MAIN COURSES

Perfect Roast Chicken

Prep: 15 mins Cook: 1 hour 20 mins Serves: 4

Ingredients:

US: 1.5kg whole chicken, 30ml olive oil, 1 lemon (halved), 4 garlic cloves (crushed), 1 tablespoon dried thyme, 1 tablespoon dried rosemary, salt, pepper

UK: 1.5kg whole chicken, 30ml olive oil, 1 lemon (halved), 4 garlic cloves (crushed), 1 tablespoon dried thyme, 1 tablespoon dried rosemary, salt, pepper

Instructions:

1. Preheat your Salter air fryer to 180°C (350°F).
2. Rinse the chicken inside and out, then pat dry with kitchen paper.
3. Rub the chicken all over with olive oil, ensuring an even coat.
4. Squeeze the lemon halves over the chicken, then place them inside the cavity along with the crushed garlic cloves.
5. Sprinkle the dried thyme, dried rosemary, salt, and pepper over the chicken, ensuring it's evenly coated.
6. Place the chicken breast side down in the air fryer basket.
7. Cook for 40 minutes, then carefully flip the chicken and cook for an additional 40 minutes or until the internal temperature reaches 75°C (165°F).
8. Let the chicken rest for 10 minutes before carving.

Nutritional Info: Calories: 320 Fat: 20g Carbs: 0g Protein: 32g

Crispy Skin Salmon

Prep: 5 mins Cook: 10 mins Serves: 2

Ingredients:

US: 2 salmon fillets (about 200g each), 1 tablespoon olive oil, salt, pepper, lemon wedges (for serving)

UK: 2 salmon fillets (about 200g each), 1 tablespoon olive oil, salt, pepper, lemon wedges (for serving)

Instructions:

1. Preheat your Salter air fryer to 200°C (390°F).
2. Brush the salmon fillets with olive oil and season with salt and pepper.
3. Place the salmon fillets skin-side down in the air fryer basket.
4. Cook for 8-10 minutes, until the skin is crispy and the salmon is cooked through.
5. Serve immediately with lemon wedges.

Nutritional Info: Calories: 280 Fat: 18g Carbs: 0g Protein: 26g

BBQ Pork Chops

Prep: 10 mins Cook: 15 mins Serves: 2

Ingredients:

US: 2 pork chops (about 250g each), 2 tablespoons BBQ sauce, 1 tablespoon olive oil, salt, pepper

UK: 2 pork chops (about 250g each), 2 tablespoons BBQ sauce, 1 tablespoon olive oil, salt, pepper

Instructions:

1. Preheat your Salter air fryer to 200°C (390°F).
2. Brush the pork chops with olive oil and season with salt and pepper.
3. Place the pork chops in the air fryer basket.
4. Cook for 10 minutes, then brush with BBQ sauce and cook for an additional 5 minutes.
5. Ensure the pork chops reach an internal temperature of 75°C (165°F).

Nutritional Info: Calories: 350 Fat: 20g Carbs: 5g Protein: 35g

Veggie Stuffed Peppers

Prep: 15 mins Cook: 20 mins Serves: 4

Ingredients:

US: 4 bell peppers (tops cut off and seeds removed), 200g cooked quinoa, 100g black beans (rinsed and drained), 100g corn kernels, 1 tomato (diced), 1 teaspoon cumin, 1 teaspoon paprika, salt, pepper, 50g shredded cheddar cheese

UK: 4 bell peppers (tops cut off and seeds removed), 200g cooked quinoa, 100g black beans (rinsed and drained), 100g corn kernels, 1 tomato (diced), 1 teaspoon cumin, 1 teaspoon paprika, salt, pepper, 50g shredded cheddar cheese

Instructions:

1. Preheat your Salter air fryer to 180°C (350°F).
2. In a bowl, combine the cooked quinoa, black beans, corn kernels, diced tomato, cumin, paprika, salt, and pepper.
3. Stuff the bell peppers with the quinoa mixture.
4. Place the stuffed peppers in the air fryer basket.
5. Cook for 15 minutes, then sprinkle with cheddar cheese and cook for an additional 5 minutes.
6. Serve hot.

Nutritional Info: Calories: 250 Fat: 8g Carbs: 35g Protein: 10g

Buttermilk Fried Chicken

Prep: 20 mins Cook: 25 mins Serves: 4

Ingredients:

US: 500g chicken thighs (bone-in, skin-on), 250ml buttermilk, 150g plain flour, 1 teaspoon paprika, 1 teaspoon garlic powder, 1 teaspoon onion powder, salt, pepper, cooking spray
UK: 500g chicken thighs (bone-in, skin-on), 250ml buttermilk, 150g plain flour, 1 teaspoon paprika, 1 teaspoon garlic powder, 1 teaspoon onion powder, salt, pepper, cooking spray

Instructions:

1. Preheat your Salter air fryer to 200°C (390°F).
2. In a bowl, marinate the chicken thighs in buttermilk for at least 1 hour.
3. In a separate bowl, combine the flour, paprika, garlic powder, onion powder, salt, and pepper.
4. Dredge the marinated chicken thighs in the flour mixture, ensuring an even coat.
5. Place the coated chicken thighs in the air fryer basket and spray lightly with cooking spray.
6. Cook for 25 minutes, turning halfway through, until golden and crispy and the internal temperature reaches 75°C (165°F).
7. Serve hot.

Nutritional Info: Calories: 400 Fat: 22g Carbs: 25g Protein: 25g

Honey Garlic Glazed Meatballs

Prep: 15 mins Cook: 15 mins Serves: 4

Ingredients:

US: 500g ground beef, 1 egg, 50g breadcrumbs, 2 garlic cloves (minced), 2 tablespoons soy sauce, 2 tablespoons honey, 1 tablespoon ketchup, 1 teaspoon ginger (grated), salt, pepper

UK: 500g ground beef, 1 egg, 50g breadcrumbs, 2 garlic cloves (minced), 2 tablespoons soy sauce, 2 tablespoons honey, 1 tablespoon ketchup, 1 teaspoon ginger (grated), salt, pepper

Instructions:

1. Preheat your Salter air fryer to 190°C (375°F).
2. In a bowl, combine the ground beef, egg, breadcrumbs, minced garlic, salt, and pepper. Mix well and form into meatballs.
3. Place the meatballs in the air fryer basket and cook for 10 minutes.
4. In a small bowl, mix the soy sauce, honey, ketchup, and grated ginger.
5. After 10 minutes, brush the meatballs with the honey garlic glaze and cook for an additional 5 minutes.
6. Serve hot with extra glaze if desired.

Nutritional Info: Calories: 300 Fat: 18g Carbs: 15g Protein: 20g

Lemon Herb Tilapia

Prep: 10 mins Cook: 12 mins Serves: 2

Ingredients:

US: 2 tilapia fillets (about 150g each), 1 lemon (sliced), 1 tablespoon olive oil, 1 teaspoon dried thyme, 1 teaspoon dried basil, salt, pepper

UK: 2 tilapia fillets (about 150g each), 1 lemon (sliced), 1 tablespoon olive oil, 1 teaspoon dried thyme, 1 teaspoon dried basil, salt, pepper

Instructions:

1. Preheat your Salter air fryer to 180°C (350°F).
2. Brush the tilapia fillets with olive oil and season with thyme, basil, salt, and pepper.
3. Place the lemon slices on top of the fillets.
4. Place the fillets in the air fryer basket.
5. Cook for 10-12 minutes, until the fish flakes easily with a fork.
6. Serve immediately.

Nutritional Info: Calories: 200 Fat: 10g Carbs: 1g Protein: 24g

Beef and Broccoli Stir Fry

Prep: 10 mins Cook: 15 mins Serves: 4

Ingredients:

US: 400g beef sirloin (thinly sliced), 250g broccoli florets, 2 tablespoons soy sauce, 1 tablespoon oyster sauce, 1 tablespoon sesame oil, 2 garlic cloves (minced), 1 teaspoon ginger (grated), 1 tablespoon cornstarch, salt, pepper

UK: 400g beef sirloin (thinly sliced), 250g broccoli florets, 2 tablespoons soy sauce, 1 tablespoon oyster sauce, 1 tablespoon sesame oil, 2 garlic cloves (minced), 1 teaspoon ginger (grated), 1 tablespoon cornstarch, salt, pepper

Instructions:

1. Preheat your Salter air fryer to 200°C (390°F).
2. In a bowl, combine the soy sauce, oyster sauce, sesame oil, minced garlic, grated ginger, and cornstarch. Mix well.
3. Toss the sliced beef in the sauce mixture until well-coated.
4. Place the beef and broccoli florets in the air fryer basket.
5. Cook for 12-15 minutes, shaking the basket halfway through.
6. Serve hot over rice.

Nutritional Info: Calories: 350 Fat: 18g Carbs: 15g Protein: 30g

Vegetarian Chickpea Curry

Prep: 10 mins Cook: 20 mins Serves: 4

Ingredients:

US: 400g canned chickpeas (rinsed and drained), 1 onion (diced), 2 garlic cloves (minced), 1 tablespoon curry powder, 400g canned tomatoes, 200ml coconut milk, 1 tablespoon olive oil, salt, pepper, fresh cilantro (for garnish)

UK: 400g canned chickpeas (rinsed and drained), 1 onion (diced), 2 garlic cloves (minced), 1 tablespoon curry powder, 400g canned tomatoes, 200ml coconut milk, 1 tablespoon olive oil, salt, pepper, fresh cilantro (for garnish)

Instructions:

1. Preheat your Salter air fryer to 180°C (350°F).
2. In a bowl, mix the chickpeas, diced onion, minced garlic, curry powder, canned tomatoes, coconut milk, olive oil, salt, and pepper.
3. Place the mixture in the air fryer basket.
4. Cook for 20 minutes, stirring halfway through.

5. Garnish with fresh cilantro before serving.

Nutritional Info: Calories: 280 Fat: 12g Carbs: 35g Protein: 10g

Parmesan Crusted Cod

Prep: 10 mins Cook: 12 mins Serves: 2

Ingredients:

US: 2 cod fillets (about 150g each), 50g grated parmesan cheese, 1 tablespoon breadcrumbs, 1 tablespoon olive oil, salt, pepper, lemon wedges (for serving)

UK: 2 cod fillets (about 150g each), 50g grated parmesan cheese, 1 tablespoon breadcrumbs, 1 tablespoon olive oil, salt, pepper, lemon wedges (for serving)

Instructions:

1. Preheat your Salter air fryer to 190°C (375°F).
2. In a bowl, combine the grated parmesan cheese and breadcrumbs.
3. Brush the cod fillets with olive oil and season with salt and pepper.
4. Press the fillets into the parmesan mixture to coat evenly.
5. Place the fillets in the air fryer basket.
6. Cook for 10-12 minutes, until the crust is golden and the fish flakes easily with a fork.
7. Serve with lemon wedges.

Nutritional Info: Calories: 250 Fat: 10g Carbs: 5g Protein: 30g

Stuffed Portobello Mushrooms

Prep: 15 mins Cook: 15 mins Serves: 4

Ingredients:

US: 4 large portobello mushrooms (stems removed), 200g cream cheese, 50g spinach (chopped), 50g grated mozzarella, 2 garlic cloves (minced), salt, pepper

UK: 4 large portobello mushrooms (stems removed), 200g cream cheese, 50g spinach (chopped), 50g grated mozzarella, 2 garlic cloves (minced), salt, pepper

Instructions:

1. Preheat your Salter air fryer to 180°C (350°F).
2. In a bowl, mix the cream cheese, chopped spinach, grated mozzarella, minced garlic, salt, and pepper.
3. Stuff the portobello mushrooms with the cream cheese mixture.
4. Place the mushrooms in the air fryer basket.
5. Cook for 15 minutes, until the mushrooms are tender and the filling is golden and bubbly.

6. Serve hot.
Nutritional Info: Calories: 220 Fat: 18g Carbs: 5g Protein: 8g

Teriyaki Chicken Skewers

Prep: 20 mins Cook: 12 mins Serves: 4

Ingredients:

US: 500g chicken breast (cut into chunks), 50ml teriyaki sauce, 1 bell pepper (cut into chunks), 1 onion (cut into chunks), 1 tablespoon sesame seeds, 1 tablespoon olive oil, salt, pepper

UK: 500g chicken breast (cut into chunks), 50ml teriyaki sauce, 1 bell pepper (cut into chunks), 1 onion (cut into chunks), 1 tablespoon sesame seeds, 1 tablespoon olive oil, salt, pepper

Instructions:

1. Preheat your Salter air fryer to 200°C (390°F).
2. In a bowl, marinate the chicken chunks in teriyaki sauce for at least 1 hour.
3. Thread the chicken, bell pepper, and onion onto skewers.
4. Brush the skewers with olive oil and season with salt and pepper.
5. Place the skewers in the air fryer basket.
6. Cook for 10-12 minutes, turning halfway through.
7. Sprinkle with sesame seeds before serving.

Nutritional Info: Calories: 300 Fat: 10g Carbs: 10g Protein: 40g

Garlic Butter Steak Bites

Prep: 10 mins Cook: 8 mins Serves: 4

Ingredients:

US: 500g sirloin steak (cut into cubes), 3 tablespoons butter (melted), 2 garlic cloves (minced), salt, pepper, chopped fresh parsley (for garnish)

UK: 500g sirloin steak (cut into cubes), 3 tablespoons butter (melted), 2 garlic cloves (minced), salt, pepper, chopped fresh parsley (for garnish)

Instructions:

1. Preheat your Salter air fryer to 200°C (390°F).
2. Toss the steak cubes with melted butter, minced garlic, salt, and pepper.
3. Place the steak bites in the air fryer basket.
4. Cook for 6-8 minutes, shaking the basket halfway through.
5. Garnish with chopped fresh parsley before serving.

Nutritional Info: Calories: 350 Fat: 25g Carbs: 0g Protein: 30g

Spinach and Ricotta Stuffed Shells

Prep: 15 mins Cook: 20 mins Serves: 4

Ingredients:

US: 200g jumbo pasta shells, 250g ricotta cheese, 100g spinach (chopped), 50g grated parmesan cheese, 1 egg, 1 garlic clove (minced), 400g marinara sauce, salt, pepper

UK: 200g jumbo pasta shells, 250g ricotta cheese, 100g spinach (chopped), 50g grated parmesan cheese, 1 egg, 1 garlic clove (minced), 400g marinara sauce, salt, pepper

Instructions:

1. Preheat your Salter air fryer to 180°C (350°F).
2. Cook the pasta shells according to package instructions, then drain and set aside.
3. In a bowl, mix the ricotta cheese, chopped spinach, grated parmesan cheese, egg, minced garlic, salt, and pepper.
4. Stuff the cooked pasta shells with the ricotta mixture.
5. Spread a layer of marinara sauce in the bottom of the air fryer basket.
6. Place the stuffed shells on top of the sauce, then spoon additional sauce over the shells.
7. Cook for 20 minutes, until the shells are heated through and the sauce is bubbling.
8. Serve hot.

Nutritional Info: Calories: 400 Fat: 18g Carbs: 40g Protein: 18g

BBQ Pulled Pork (for reheating)

Prep: 5 mins Cook: 10 mins Serves: 4

Ingredients:

US: 500g cooked pulled pork, 100ml BBQ sauce, 4 burger buns

UK: 500g cooked pulled pork, 100ml BBQ sauce, 4 burger buns

Instructions:

1. Preheat your Salter air fryer to 180°C (350°F).
2. In a bowl, mix the cooked pulled pork with BBQ sauce.
3. Place the pulled pork in the air fryer basket.
4. Cook for 8-10 minutes, stirring halfway through, until heated through.
5. Serve the pulled pork on burger buns.

Nutritional Info: Calories: 450 Fat: 20g Carbs: 40g Protein: 25g

CHAPTER 4: VIBRANT VEGETABLE SIDES

Crispy Brussels Sprouts

Prep: 10 mins Cook: 15 mins Serves: 4

Ingredients:

US: 500g Brussels sprouts (halved), 30ml olive oil, 1 teaspoon garlic powder, salt, pepper, 2 tablespoons grated Parmesan cheese

UK: 500g Brussels sprouts (halved), 30ml olive oil, 1 teaspoon garlic powder, salt, pepper, 2 tablespoons grated Parmesan cheese

Instructions:

1. Preheat your Salter Air Fryer to 200°C (392°F).
2. In a bowl, toss the halved Brussels sprouts with olive oil, garlic powder, salt, and pepper until well coated.
3. Place the Brussels sprouts in the air fryer basket in a single layer.
4. Cook for 12-15 minutes, shaking the basket halfway through, until crispy and golden brown.
5. Remove from the air fryer and sprinkle with grated Parmesan cheese.
6. Serve immediately for a delicious and healthy side dish.

Nutritional Info: Calories: 120 Fat: 8g Carbs: 10g Protein: 4g

Parmesan Roasted Broccoli

Prep: 10 mins Cook: 10 mins Serves: 4

Ingredients:

US: 500g broccoli florets, 30ml olive oil, 2 tablespoons grated Parmesan cheese, 1 teaspoon garlic powder, salt, pepper

UK: 500g broccoli florets, 30ml olive oil, 2 tablespoons grated Parmesan cheese, 1 teaspoon garlic powder, salt, pepper

Instructions:

1. Preheat your Salter Air Fryer to 200°C (392°F).
2. In a bowl, toss the broccoli florets with olive oil, grated Parmesan, garlic powder, salt, and pepper.
3. Place the broccoli in the air fryer basket in a single layer.
4. Cook for 8-10 minutes, shaking the basket halfway through, until the broccoli is tender and crispy.
5. Serve immediately for a cheesy, garlicky vegetable side.

Nutritional Info: Calories: 130 Fat: 9g Carbs: 9g Protein: 4g

Honey Glazed Carrots

Prep: 10 mins Cook: 15 mins Serves: 4

Ingredients:

US: 500g carrots (peeled and sliced into sticks), 30ml olive oil, 2 tablespoons honey, 1 tablespoon balsamic vinegar, salt, pepper, chopped fresh parsley (for garnish)

UK: 500g carrots (peeled and sliced into sticks), 30ml olive oil, 2 tablespoons honey, 1 tablespoon balsamic vinegar, salt, pepper, chopped fresh parsley (for garnish)

Instructions:

1. Preheat your Salter Air Fryer to 180°C (356°F).
2. In a bowl, toss the carrot sticks with olive oil, honey, balsamic vinegar, salt, and pepper until well coated.
3. Place the glazed carrots in the air fryer basket in a single layer.
4. Cook for 12-15 minutes, shaking the basket halfway through, until the carrots are tender and caramelized.
5. Remove from the air fryer and transfer to a serving platter.
6. Garnish with chopped fresh parsley before serving.

Nutritional Info: Calories: 150 Fat: 7g Carbs: 20g Protein: 2g

Garlic Green Beans

Prep: 10 mins Cook: 10 mins Serves: 4

Ingredients:

US: 500g green beans (trimmed), 30ml olive oil, 3 cloves garlic (minced), salt, pepper
UK: 500g green beans (trimmed), 30ml olive oil, 3 cloves garlic (minced), salt, pepper

Instructions:

1. Preheat your Salter Air Fryer to 190°C (374°F).
2. In a bowl, toss the green beans with olive oil, minced garlic, salt, and pepper.
3. Place the green beans in the air fryer basket in a single layer.
4. Cook for 8-10 minutes, shaking the basket halfway through, until the beans are tender and slightly crispy.
5. Serve immediately for a simple and flavorful side dish.

Nutritional Info: Calories: 110 Fat: 7g Carbs: 10g Protein: 2g

Crispy Kale Chips

Prep: 5 mins Cook: 10 mins Serves: 4

Ingredients:

US: 200g kale leaves (stems removed, torn into bite-sized pieces), 15ml olive oil, salt, pepper
UK: 200g kale leaves (stems removed, torn into bite-sized pieces), 15ml olive oil, salt, pepper

Instructions:

1. Preheat your Salter Air Fryer to 180°C (356°F).
2. In a bowl, toss the kale pieces with olive oil, salt, and pepper until evenly coated.
3. Place the kale in the air fryer basket in a single layer.
4. Cook for 8-10 minutes, shaking the basket halfway through, until the kale is crispy.
5. Serve immediately for a healthy and crunchy snack.

Nutritional Info: Calories: 50 Fat: 3g Carbs: 5g Protein: 2g

Rosemary Roasted Potatoes

Prep: 10 mins Cook: 20 mins Serves: 4

Ingredients:

US: 500g baby potatoes (halved), 30ml olive oil, 1 teaspoon dried rosemary, salt, pepper
UK: 500g baby potatoes (halved), 30ml olive oil, 1 teaspoon dried rosemary, salt, pepper

Instructions:

1. Preheat your Salter Air Fryer to 200°C (392°F).
2. In a bowl, toss the halved baby potatoes with olive oil, dried rosemary, salt, and pepper.
3. Place the potatoes in the air fryer basket in a single layer.
4. Cook for 18-20 minutes, shaking the basket halfway through, until the potatoes are golden and crispy.
5. Serve immediately for a delicious and aromatic side dish.

Nutritional Info: Calories: 150 Fat: 7g Carbs: 20g Protein: 2g

Spicy Cauliflower Wings

Prep: 10 mins Cook: 20 mins Serves: 4

Ingredients:

US: 1 large cauliflower (cut into florets), 30ml olive oil, 1 teaspoon smoked paprika, 1 teaspoon garlic powder, 1/2 teaspoon cayenne pepper, salt, pepper

UK: 1 large cauliflower (cut into florets), 30ml olive oil, 1 teaspoon smoked paprika, 1 teaspoon garlic powder, 1/2 teaspoon cayenne pepper, salt, pepper

Instructions:

1. Preheat your Salter Air Fryer to 200°C (392°F).
2. In a bowl, toss the cauliflower florets with olive oil, smoked paprika, garlic powder, cayenne pepper, salt, and pepper.
3. Place the cauliflower in the air fryer basket in a single layer.
4. Cook for 18-20 minutes, shaking the basket halfway through, until tender and crispy.
5. Serve with a cooling dip like ranch or blue cheese.

Nutritional Info: Calories: 100 Fat: 7g Carbs: 8g Protein: 3g

Parmesan Zucchini Fries

Prep: 10 mins Cook: 15 mins Serves: 4

Ingredients:

US: 2 medium zucchinis (cut into sticks), 30ml olive oil, 2 tablespoons grated Parmesan cheese, 1 teaspoon garlic powder, salt, pepper

UK: 2 medium courgettes (cut into sticks), 30ml olive oil, 2 tablespoons grated Parmesan cheese, 1 teaspoon garlic powder, salt, pepper

Instructions:

1. Preheat your Salter Air Fryer to 200°C (392°F).
2. In a bowl, toss the zucchini sticks with olive oil, grated Parmesan, garlic powder, salt, and pepper.
3. Place the zucchini in the air fryer basket in a single layer.
4. Cook for 12-15 minutes, shaking the basket halfway through, until crispy and golden.
5. Serve immediately with your favourite dipping sauce.

Nutritional Info: Calories: 120 Fat: 7g Carbs: 10g Protein: 3g

Crispy Onion Rings

Prep: 15 mins Cook: 10 mins Serves: 4

Ingredients:

US: 2 large onions (sliced into rings), 50g flour, 2 large eggs (beaten), 100g breadcrumbs, 1 teaspoon paprika, salt, pepper, olive oil spray

UK: 2 large onions (sliced into rings), 50g flour, 2 large eggs (beaten), 100g breadcrumbs, 1 teaspoon paprika, salt, pepper, olive oil spray

Instructions:

1. Preheat your Salter Air Fryer to 200°C (392°F).
2. Set up a breading station with flour, beaten eggs, and breadcrumbs mixed with paprika, salt, and pepper.
3. Dip each onion ring in flour, then egg, and finally coat with breadcrumbs.
4. Arrange the onion rings in the air fryer basket and spray lightly with olive oil.
5. Cook for 8-10 minutes, turning halfway through, until golden and crispy.
6. Serve immediately with your favourite dipping sauce.

Nutritional Info: Calories: 180 Fat: 7g Carbs: 25g Protein: 4g

Maple Roasted Butternut Squash

Prep: 10 mins Cook: 20 mins Serves: 4

Ingredients:

US: 500g butternut squash (peeled and cubed), 30ml olive oil, 2 tablespoons maple syrup, 1 teaspoon cinnamon, salt, pepper

UK: 500g butternut squash (peeled and cubed), 30ml olive oil, 2 tablespoons maple syrup, 1 teaspoon cinnamon, salt, pepper

Instructions:

1. Preheat your Salter Air Fryer to 200°C (392°F).
2. In a bowl, toss the butternut squash cubes with olive oil, maple syrup, cinnamon, salt, and pepper.
3. Place the squash in the air fryer basket in a single layer.
4. Cook for 18-20 minutes, shaking the basket halfway through, until tender and caramelized.
5. Serve immediately for a sweet and savoury side dish.

Nutritional Info: Calories: 140 Fat: 7g Carbs: 20g Protein: 2g

Crispy Okra

Prep: 10 mins | Cook: 12 mins | Serves: 4

Ingredients:

US: 500g okra (sliced lengthwise), 30ml olive oil, 50g cornmeal, 1 teaspoon garlic powder, 1 teaspoon paprika, salt, pepper

UK: 500g okra (sliced lengthwise), 30ml olive oil, 50g cornmeal, 1 teaspoon garlic powder, 1 teaspoon paprika, salt, pepper

Instructions:

1. Preheat your Salter Air Fryer to 200°C (392°F).
2. In a bowl, toss the sliced okra with olive oil, garlic powder, paprika, salt, and pepper until well coated.
3. Coat the okra in cornmeal.
4. Place the okra in the air fryer basket in a single layer.
5. Cook for 10-12 minutes, shaking the basket halfway through, until the okra is crispy and golden.
6. Serve immediately.

Nutritional Info: Calories: 130 | Fat: 7g | Carbs: 16g | Protein: 3g

Garlic Mushroom Caps

Prep: 10 mins | Cook: 10 mins | Serves: 4

Ingredients:

US: 500g large mushrooms (stems removed), 30ml olive oil, 3 cloves garlic (minced), 1 teaspoon dried thyme, salt, pepper

UK: 500g large mushrooms (stems removed), 30ml olive oil, 3 cloves garlic (minced), 1 teaspoon dried thyme, salt, pepper

Instructions:

1. Preheat your Salter Air Fryer to 190°C (374°F).
2. In a bowl, toss the mushroom caps with olive oil, minced garlic, dried thyme, salt, and pepper until well coated.
3. Place the mushrooms in the air fryer basket in a single layer.
4. Cook for 8-10 minutes, shaking the basket halfway through, until the mushrooms are tender and juicy.
5. Serve immediately.

Nutritional Info: Calories: 100 | Fat: 7g | Carbs: 5g | Protein: 3g

Sesame Asparagus Spears

Prep: 5 mins | Cook: 10 mins | Serves: 4

Ingredients:

US: 500g asparagus spears (trimmed), 30ml olive oil, 2 tablespoons sesame seeds, salt, pepper

UK: 500g asparagus spears (trimmed), 30ml olive oil, 2 tablespoons sesame seeds, salt, pepper

Instructions:

1. Preheat your Salter Air Fryer to 190°C (374°F).

2. In a bowl, toss the asparagus spears with olive oil, sesame seeds, salt, and pepper until well coated.

3. Place the asparagus in the air fryer basket in a single layer.

4. Cook for 8-10 minutes, shaking the basket halfway through, until the asparagus is tender and slightly crispy.

5. Serve immediately.

Nutritional Info: Calories: 80 | Fat: 6g | Carbs: 4g | Protein: 2g

Buffalo Cauliflower Bites

Prep: 10 mins | Cook: 15 mins | Serves: 4

Ingredients:

US: 1 large cauliflower (cut into florets), 30ml olive oil, 50g hot sauce, 1 teaspoon garlic powder, 1 teaspoon paprika, salt, pepper

UK: 1 large cauliflower (cut into florets), 30ml olive oil, 50g hot sauce, 1 teaspoon garlic powder, 1 teaspoon paprika, salt, pepper

Instructions:

1. Preheat your Salter Air Fryer to 200°C (392°F).

2. In a bowl, toss the cauliflower florets with olive oil, hot sauce, garlic powder, paprika, salt, and pepper until well coated.

3. Place the cauliflower in the air fryer basket in a single layer.

4. Cook for 12-15 minutes, shaking the basket halfway through, until the cauliflower is crispy and golden.

5. Serve immediately.

Nutritional Info: Calories: 120 | Fat: 6g | Carbs: 14g | Protein: 4g

Crispy Eggplant Rounds

Prep: 10 mins | Cook: 15 mins | Serves: 4

Ingredients:

US: 1 large eggplant (sliced into rounds), 30ml olive oil, 50g breadcrumbs, 50g grated Parmesan cheese, 1 teaspoon garlic powder, salt, pepper

UK: 1 large aubergine (sliced into rounds), 30ml olive oil, 50g breadcrumbs, 50g grated Parmesan cheese, 1 teaspoon garlic powder, salt, pepper

Instructions:

1. Preheat your Salter Air Fryer to 200°C (392°F).

2. In a bowl, toss the eggplant rounds with olive oil, garlic powder, salt, and pepper.

3. Mix breadcrumbs and grated Parmesan cheese in a separate bowl.

4. Coat the eggplant rounds in the breadcrumb and Parmesan mixture.

5. Place the eggplant rounds in the air fryer basket in a single layer.

6. Cook for 12-15 minutes, shaking the basket halfway through, until the eggplant is crispy and golden.

7. Serve immediately.

Nutritional Info: Calories: 180 | Fat: 10g | Carbs: 16g | Protein: 6g

Crispy Vegetable Samosas

Prep: 20 mins Cook: 15 mins Serves: 4

Ingredients:

US: 200g potatoes (peeled and diced), 100g peas, 1 onion (finely chopped), 2 garlic cloves (minced), 1 teaspoon cumin seeds, 1 teaspoon garam masala, 1 teaspoon turmeric, 1 teaspoon coriander powder, 1 tablespoon olive oil, 8 sheets phyllo pastry, salt, pepper

UK: 200g potatoes (peeled and diced), 100g peas, 1 onion (finely chopped), 2 garlic cloves (minced), 1 teaspoon cumin seeds, 1 teaspoon garam masala, 1 teaspoon turmeric, 1 teaspoon coriander powder, 1 tablespoon olive oil, 8 sheets phyllo pastry, salt, pepper

Instructions:

1. Preheat your Salter air fryer to 180°C (350°F).
2. Boil the diced potatoes until tender, then drain and set aside.
3. In a pan, heat the olive oil over medium heat. Add the cumin seeds and fry for a minute until fragrant.
4. Add the chopped onion and garlic, cooking until soft.
5. Stir in the garam masala, turmeric, coriander powder, salt, and pepper. Cook for another minute.
6. Add the boiled potatoes and peas to the pan, mixing well. Cook for 5 minutes, then let the mixture cool.
7. Cut each phyllo pastry sheet into strips. Place a spoonful of the filling at the end of each strip and fold it into triangles.
8. Place the samosas in the air fryer basket and cook for 15 minutes, until golden and crispy.
9. Serve hot with your favourite chutney.

Nutritional Info: Calories: 150 Fat: 5g Carbs: 25g Protein: 3g

Mini Beef Empanadas

Prep: 25 mins Cook: 20 mins Serves: 4

Ingredients:

US: 300g ground beef, 1 onion (finely chopped), 1 garlic clove (minced), 1 red bell pepper (diced), 1 teaspoon paprika, 1 teaspoon cumin, 1 tablespoon tomato paste, 1 tablespoon olive oil, 1 pack refrigerated pie crusts (about 400g), salt, pepper

UK: 300g ground beef, 1 onion (finely chopped), 1 garlic clove (minced), 1 red bell pepper (diced), 1 teaspoon paprika, 1 teaspoon cumin, 1 tablespoon tomato paste, 1 tablespoon olive oil, 1 pack refrigerated pie crusts (about 400g), salt, pepper

Instructions:

1. Preheat your Salter air fryer to 190°C (375°F).
2. In a pan, heat the olive oil over medium heat. Add the onion and garlic, cooking until soft.
3. Add the ground beef, breaking it up as it cooks until browned.
4. Stir in the diced bell pepper, paprika, cumin, tomato paste, salt, and pepper. Cook for another 5 minutes.
5. Roll out the pie crusts and cut into small circles using a cookie cutter.
6. Place a spoonful of the beef mixture in the centre of each circle, fold over, and seal the edges with a fork.
7. Place the empanadas in the air fryer basket and cook for 20 minutes, until golden and crispy.
8. Serve hot with salsa or sour cream.

Nutritional Info: Calories: 300 Fat: 15g Carbs: 30g Protein: 10g

Falafel Bites

Prep: 15 mins Cook: 12 mins Serves: 4

Ingredients:

US: 400g canned chickpeas (drained and rinsed), 1 onion (finely chopped), 2 garlic cloves (minced), 1 teaspoon ground cumin, 1 teaspoon ground coriander, 1 teaspoon baking powder, 2 tablespoons flour, 1 tablespoon olive oil, salt, pepper, fresh parsley (for garnish)

UK: 400g canned chickpeas (drained and rinsed), 1 onion (finely chopped), 2 garlic cloves (minced), 1 teaspoon ground cumin, 1 teaspoon ground coriander, 1 teaspoon baking powder, 2 tablespoons flour, 1 tablespoon olive oil, salt, pepper, fresh parsley (for garnish)

Instructions:

1. Preheat your Salter air fryer to 180°C (350°F).
2. In a food processor, combine the chickpeas, onion, garlic, cumin, coriander, baking powder, flour, salt, and pepper. Pulse until smooth.
3. Form the mixture into small balls.
4. Place the falafel balls in the air fryer basket and brush lightly with olive oil.
5. Cook for 12 minutes, shaking the basket halfway through.
6. Garnish with fresh parsley and serve with hummus or tahini sauce.

Nutritional Info: Calories: 200 Fat: 8g Carbs: 25g Protein: 6g

Greek Spanakopita Triangles

Prep: 20 mins Cook: 15 mins Serves: 4

Ingredients:

US: 200g spinach (chopped), 100g feta cheese (crumbled), 1 onion (finely chopped), 2 garlic cloves (minced), 1 egg (beaten), 8 sheets phyllo pastry, 1 tablespoon olive oil, salt, pepper

UK: 200g spinach (chopped), 100g feta cheese (crumbled), 1 onion (finely chopped), 2 garlic cloves (minced), 1 egg (beaten), 8 sheets phyllo pastry, 1 tablespoon olive oil, salt, pepper

Instructions:

1. Preheat your Salter air fryer to 180°C (350°F).
2. In a pan, heat the olive oil over medium heat. Add the onion and garlic, cooking until soft.
3. In a bowl, combine the cooked onion and garlic with the chopped spinach, crumbled feta cheese, and beaten egg. Season with salt and pepper.
4. Cut each phyllo pastry sheet into strips. Place a spoonful of the filling at the end of each strip and fold it into triangles.
5. Place the spanakopita triangles in the air fryer basket and cook for 15 minutes, until golden and crispy.
6. Serve hot.

Nutritional Info: Calories: 180 Fat: 10g Carbs: 20g Protein: 5g

Chinese Crispy Duck

Prep: 20 mins Cook: 30 mins Serves: 4

Ingredients:

US: 1 duck breast (about 500g), 2 tablespoons soy sauce, 1 tablespoon hoisin sauce, 1 tablespoon honey, 1 teaspoon five-spice powder, 1 teaspoon garlic powder, 1 teaspoon ginger powder, salt, pepper

UK: 1 duck breast (about 500g), 2 tablespoons soy sauce, 1 tablespoon hoisin sauce, 1 tablespoon honey, 1 teaspoon five-spice powder, 1 teaspoon garlic powder, 1 teaspoon ginger powder, salt, pepper

Instructions:

1. Preheat your Salter air fryer to 200°C (390°F).
2. Score the duck breast skin in a criss-cross pattern.
3. In a bowl, mix the soy sauce, hoisin sauce, honey, five-spice powder, garlic powder, ginger powder, salt, and pepper.
4. Rub the mixture all over the duck breast.
5. Place the duck breast skin-side down in the air fryer basket.
6. Cook for 20 minutes, then flip and cook for another 10 minutes.
7. Let the duck rest for 5 minutes before slicing.
8. Serve hot with pancakes and hoisin sauce.

Nutritional Info: Calories: 450 Fat: 30g Carbs: 10g Protein: 25g

Mexican Street Corn

Prep: 10 mins Cook: 12 mins Serves: 4

Ingredients:

US: 4 ears of corn, 50g mayonnaise, 50g sour cream, 1 teaspoon chilli powder, 1 lime (cut into wedges), 50g grated parmesan cheese, 1 tablespoon chopped fresh cilantro, salt, pepper

UK: 4 ears of corn, 50g mayonnaise, 50g sour cream, 1 teaspoon chilli powder, 1 lime (cut into wedges), 50g grated parmesan cheese, 1 tablespoon chopped fresh cilantro, salt, pepper

Instructions:

1. Preheat your Salter air fryer to 200°C (390°F).
2. Brush the ears of corn with mayonnaise.
3. Place the corn in the air fryer basket and cook for 12 minutes, turning halfway through.
4. In a bowl, mix the sour cream, chilli powder, salt, and pepper.
5. Once the corn is cooked, brush with the sour cream mixture.
6. Sprinkle with grated parmesan cheese and chopped cilantro.
7. Serve hot with lime wedges.

Nutritional Info: Calories: 220 Fat: 12g Carbs: 25g Protein: 6g

Italian Arancini Balls

Prep: 25 mins Cook: 15 mins Serves: 4

Ingredients:

US: 300g cooked risotto, 50g mozzarella cheese (cubed), 1 egg (beaten), 50g breadcrumbs, 2 tablespoons flour, 1 tablespoon olive oil, salt, pepper

UK: 300g cooked risotto,
 50g mozzarella cheese (cubed), 1 egg (beaten), 50g breadcrumbs, 2 tablespoons flour, 1 tablespoon olive oil, salt, pepper

Instructions:

1. Preheat your Salter air fryer to 180°C (350°F).
2. Take a spoonful of cooked risotto and place a cube of mozzarella in the centre. Form into a ball.
3. Roll each ball in flour, then dip in beaten egg, and finally coat with breadcrumbs.
4. Place the arancini balls in the air fryer basket and brush lightly with olive oil.
5. Cook for 15 minutes, until golden and crispy.
6. Serve hot with marinara sauce.

Nutritional Info: Calories: 250 Fat: 10g Carbs: 30g Protein: 8g

Japanese Gyoza

Prep: 20 mins Cook: 10 mins Serves: 4

Ingredients:

US: 200g ground pork, 1 garlic clove (minced), 1 teaspoon ginger (grated), 1 spring onion (finely chopped), 1 tablespoon soy sauce, 1 teaspoon sesame oil, 20 gyoza wrappers, 1 tablespoon olive oil
UK: 200g ground pork, 1 garlic clove (minced), 1 teaspoon ginger (grated), 1 spring onion (finely chopped), 1 tablespoon soy sauce, 1 teaspoon sesame oil, 20 gyoza wrappers, 1 tablespoon olive oil

Instructions:

1. Preheat your Salter air fryer to 190°C (375°F).
2. In a bowl, mix the ground pork, minced garlic, grated ginger, chopped spring onion, soy sauce, and sesame oil.
3. Place a teaspoon of the pork mixture in the centre of each gyoza wrapper.
4. Fold the wrappers and seal the edges with a little water.
5. Brush the gyoza with olive oil and place it in the air fryer basket.
6. Cook for 10 minutes, until crispy and golden.
7. Serve hot with soy sauce for dipping.

Nutritional Info: Calories: 150 Fat: 8g Carbs: 15g Protein: 7g

Thai Fish Cakes

Prep: 15 mins Cook: 10 mins Serves: 4

Ingredients:

US: 300g white fish fillets (chopped), 1 tablespoon red curry paste, 1 egg, 1 tablespoon fish sauce, 1 tablespoon lime juice, 1 teaspoon sugar, 1 handful green beans (chopped), 1 tablespoon olive oil
UK: 300g white fish fillets (chopped), 1 tablespoon red curry paste, 1 egg, 1 tablespoon fish sauce, 1 tablespoon lime juice, 1 teaspoon sugar, 1 handful green beans (chopped), 1 tablespoon olive oil

Instructions:

1. Preheat your Salter air fryer to 180°C (350°F).
2. In a food processor, blend the fish fillets, red curry paste, egg, fish sauce, lime juice, and sugar until smooth.
3. Stir in the chopped green beans.
4. Form the mixture into small patties.
5. Brush the patties with olive oil and place in the air fryer basket.
6. Cook for 10 minutes, flipping halfway through.
7. Serve hot with sweet chilli sauce.

Nutritional Info: Calories: 200 Fat: 10g Carbs: 5g Protein: 20g

German Schnitzel

Prep: 15 mins Cook: 12 mins Serves: 4

Ingredients:

US: 4 pork cutlets (about 150g each), 50g flour, 2 eggs (beaten), 100g breadcrumbs, 1 teaspoon paprika, 1 tablespoon olive oil, salt, pepper

UK: 4 pork cutlets (about 150g each), 50g flour, 2 eggs (beaten), 100g breadcrumbs, 1 teaspoon paprika, 1 tablespoon olive oil, salt, pepper

Instructions:

1. Preheat your Salter air fryer to 190°C (375°F).
2. Season the pork cutlets with salt, pepper, and paprika.
3. Dredge each cutlet in flour, dip in beaten eggs, and coat with breadcrumbs.
4. Brush the cutlets with olive oil and place them in the air fryer basket.
5. Cook for 10-12 minutes, flipping halfway through.
6. Serve hot with lemon wedges and a side salad.

Nutritional Info: Calories: 300 Fat: 12g Carbs: 20g Protein: 25g

Indian Tandoori Chicken

Prep: 15 mins Cook: 25 mins Serves: 4

Ingredients:

US: 500g chicken thighs (skinless and boneless), 100g yoghurt, 1 tablespoon tandoori masala, 1 teaspoon garlic paste, 1 teaspoon ginger paste, 1 tablespoon lemon juice, salt, pepper

UK: 500g chicken thighs (skinless and boneless), 100g yoghurt, 1 tablespoon tandoori masala, 1 teaspoon garlic paste, 1 teaspoon ginger paste, 1 tablespoon lemon juice, salt, pepper

Instructions:

1. Preheat your Salter air fryer to 200°C (390°F).
2. In a bowl, mix the yoghurt, tandoori masala, garlic paste, ginger paste, lemon juice, salt, and pepper.
3. Coat the chicken thighs in the marinade and let sit for at least 1 hour.
4. Place the chicken thighs in the air fryer basket.
5. Cook for 20-25 minutes, until cooked through and slightly charred.
6. Serve hot with naan bread and a cucumber salad.

Nutritional Info: Calories: 320 Fat: 18g Carbs: 5g Protein: 30g

Korean Bibimbap Bowl

Prep: 20 mins Cook: 15 mins Serves: 4

Ingredients:

US: 200g beef mince, 1 carrot (julienned), 1 cucumber (julienned), 100g spinach, 4 eggs, 4 cups cooked rice, 2 tablespoons gochujang (Korean chilli paste), 1 tablespoon soy sauce, 1 tablespoon sesame oil, salt, pepper

UK: 200g beef mince, 1 carrot (julienned), 1 cucumber (julienned), 100g spinach, 4 eggs, 4 cups cooked rice, 2 tablespoons gochujang (Korean chilli paste), 1 tablespoon soy sauce, 1 tablespoon sesame oil, salt, pepper

Instructions:

1. Preheat your Salter air fryer to 180°C (350°F).
2. Cook the beef mince in a pan with soy sauce, sesame oil, salt, and pepper until browned.
3. In a bowl, arrange the cooked rice, beef mince, carrot, cucumber, and spinach.
4. Cook the eggs in the air fryer for 5 minutes, until the whites are set but the yolks are still runny.
5. Place the cooked eggs on top of the bibimbap bowls.
6. Add a spoonful of gochujang to each bowl and mix well before eating.

Nutritional Info: Calories: 450 Fat: 15g Carbs: 50g Protein: 20g

Lebanese Kibbeh

Prep: 30 mins Cook: 15 mins Serves: 4

Ingredients:

US: 200g bulgur wheat, 300g ground lamb, 1 onion (finely chopped), 1 garlic clove (minced), 1 teaspoon allspice, 1 teaspoon cinnamon, 1 tablespoon pine nuts, 1 tablespoon olive oil, salt, pepper

UK: 200g bulgur wheat, 300g ground lamb, 1 onion (finely chopped), 1 garlic clove (minced), 1 teaspoon allspice, 1 teaspoon cinnamon, 1 tablespoon pine nuts, 1 tablespoon olive oil, salt, pepper

Instructions:

1. Preheat your Salter air fryer to 180°C (350°F).
2. Soak the bulgur wheat in water for 30 minutes, then drain and squeeze out excess water.
3. In a bowl, mix the ground lamb, chopped onion, minced garlic, allspice, cinnamon, pine nuts, salt, and pepper.
4. Add the soaked bulgur wheat to the meat mixture and combine well.
5. Form the mixture into small patties.
6. Brush the patties with olive oil and place in the air fryer basket.
7. Cook for 15 minutes, flipping halfway through.

8. Serve hot with a yoghurt dip.

Nutritional Info: Calories: 300 Fat: 18g Carbs: 20g Protein: 15g

Vietnamese Spring Rolls

Prep: 20 mins Cook: 8 mins Serves: 4

Ingredients:

US: 100g rice noodles, 8 rice paper wrappers, 100g shrimp (cooked and sliced), 1 carrot (julienned), 1 cucumber (julienned), 1 handful mint leaves, 1 handful cilantro, 1 tablespoon soy sauce, 1 tablespoon hoisin sauce

UK: 100g rice noodles, 8 rice paper wrappers, 100g shrimp (cooked and sliced), 1 carrot (julienned), 1 cucumber (julienned), 1 handful mint leaves, 1 handful cilantro, 1 tablespoon soy sauce, 1 tablespoon hoisin sauce

Instructions:

1. Preheat your Salter air fryer to 180°C (350°F).
2. Cook the rice noodles according to package instructions and set aside.
3. Soak the rice paper wrappers in warm water until soft.
4. On each wrapper, place a small number of noodles, shrimp, carrots, cucumber, mint leaves, and cilantro.
5. Roll the wrapper tightly around the filling.
6. Brush the spring rolls lightly with olive oil and place in the air fryer basket.
7. Cook for 8 minutes, turning halfway through.
8. Serve hot with soy sauce and hoisin sauce for dipping.

Nutritional Info: Calories: 150 Fat: 3g Carbs: 25g Protein: 6g

American Buffalo Chicken Tenders

Prep: 15 mins Cook: 10 mins Serves: 4

Ingredients:

US: 400g chicken tenders, 50g flour, 2 eggs (beaten), 100g breadcrumbs, 50g buffalo sauce, 1 tablespoon olive oil, salt, pepper

UK: 400g chicken tenders, 50g flour, 2 eggs (beaten), 100g breadcrumbs, 50g buffalo sauce, 1 tablespoon olive oil, salt, pepper

Instructions:

1. Preheat your Salter air fryer to 200°C (390°F).
2. Season the chicken tenders with salt and pepper.
3. Dredge each tender in flour, dip in beaten eggs, and coat with breadcrumbs.
4. Brush the tenders with olive oil and place in the air fryer basket.
5. Cook for 10 minutes, flipping halfway through.
6. Toss the cooked tenders in buffalo sauce.
7. Serve hot with ranch dressing and celery sticks.

Nutritional Info: Calories: 300 Fat: 12g Carbs: 20g Protein: 25g

CHAPTER 6: GUILT-FREE FAVOURITE

Skinny Fish and Chips

Prep: 15 mins Cook: 20 mins Serves: 4

Ingredients:

US: 500g cod fillets (cut into strips), 500g potatoes (cut into chips), 30ml olive oil, 100g whole wheat breadcrumbs, 2 large eggs (beaten), 1 teaspoon paprika, salt, pepper, lemon wedges (for serving)

UK: 500g cod fillets (cut into strips), 500g potatoes (cut into chips), 30ml olive oil, 100g whole wheat breadcrumbs, 2 large eggs (beaten), 1 teaspoon paprika, salt, pepper, lemon wedges (for serving)

Instructions:

1. Preheat your Salter Air Fryer to 200°C (392°F).
2. Toss the potato chips in olive oil, salt, and pepper, and place them in the air fryer basket. Cook for 10 minutes, shaking the basket halfway through.
3. Set up a breading station with beaten eggs and breadcrumbs mixed with paprika, salt, and pepper.
4. Dip each cod strip in the egg, then coat it with breadcrumbs.
5. After the chips have cooked for 10 minutes, add the breaded cod strips to the air fryer basket.
6. Cook for an additional 10 minutes, shaking the basket halfway through, until the fish is crispy and the chips are golden.
7. Serve immediately with lemon wedges and a side of tartar sauce, if desired.

Nutritional Info: Calories: 350 Fat: 10g Carbs: 40g Protein: 25g

Crispy Chicken Tenders

Prep: 10 mins Cook: 15 mins Serves: 4

Ingredients:

US: 500g chicken tenders, 30ml olive oil, 100g whole wheat breadcrumbs, 2 large eggs (beaten), 1 teaspoon garlic powder, 1 teaspoon paprika, salt, pepper

UK: 500g chicken tenders, 30ml olive oil, 100g whole wheat breadcrumbs, 2 large eggs (beaten), 1 teaspoon garlic powder, 1 teaspoon paprika, salt, pepper

Instructions:

1. Preheat your Salter Air Fryer to 200°C (392°F).
2. Set up a breading station with beaten eggs and breadcrumbs mixed with garlic powder, paprika, salt, and pepper.
3. Dip each chicken tender in the egg, then coat with the breadcrumb mixture.
4. Place the breaded chicken tenders in the air fryer basket in a single layer.
5. Cook for 12-15 minutes, shaking the basket halfway through, until the chicken is golden and cooked through.
6. Serve immediately with your favourite dipping sauce.

Nutritional Info: Calories: 300 Fat: 12g Carbs: 20g Protein: 25g

Low-Carb Cauliflower Pizza

Prep: 15 mins Cook: 20 mins Serves: 2

Ingredients:

US: 1 medium cauliflower (grated), 100g mozzarella cheese (shredded), 1 large egg, 1 teaspoon dried oregano, 50ml tomato sauce, 50g mozzarella cheese (shredded, for topping), salt, pepper, fresh basil (for garnish)

UK: 1 medium cauliflower (grated), 100g mozzarella cheese (shredded), 1 large egg, 1 teaspoon dried oregano, 50ml tomato sauce, 50g mozzarella cheese (shredded, for topping), salt, pepper, fresh basil (for garnish)

Instructions:

1. Preheat your Salter Air Fryer to 180°C (356°F).
2. In a bowl, mix the grated cauliflower, shredded mozzarella, egg, oregano, salt, and pepper until well combined.
3. Shape the mixture into a pizza crust on a piece of parchment paper.
4. Place the crust in the air fryer basket and cook for 10 minutes.
5. Remove the crust, spread with tomato sauce, and top with additional shredded mozzarella.
6. Return to the air fryer and cook for another 8-10 minutes until the cheese is melted and bubbly.
7. Garnish with fresh basil before serving.

Nutritional Info: Calories: 250 Fat: 15g Carbs: 10g Protein: 20g

Veggie Loaded Frittata

Prep: 10 mins Cook: 15 mins Serves: 4

Ingredients:

US: 6 large eggs, 100ml milk, 100g bell peppers (chopped), 100g spinach (chopped), 50g feta cheese (crumbled), salt, pepper, 1 teaspoon olive oil

UK: 6 large eggs, 100ml milk, 100g bell peppers (chopped), 100g spinach (chopped), 50g feta cheese (crumbled), salt, pepper, 1 teaspoon olive oil

Instructions:

1. Preheat your Salter Air Fryer to 180°C (356°F).
2. In a bowl, whisk together the eggs, milk, salt, and pepper.
3. Stir in the chopped bell peppers, spinach, and feta cheese.
4. Grease a baking dish with olive oil and pour in the egg mixture.
5. Place the dish in the air fryer basket and cook for 12-15 minutes, until the frittata is set and golden.
6. Serve warm as a nutritious and delicious breakfast or brunch option.

Nutritional Info: Calories: 200 Fat: 15g Carbs: 5g Protein: 15g

Zucchini Nachos

Prep: 10 mins Cook: 15 mins Serves: 4

Ingredients:

US: 2 large zucchinis (sliced into rounds), 30ml olive oil, 100g shredded cheddar cheese, 1 jalapeño (sliced), 50g black beans, 2 tablespoons sour cream, 2 tablespoons salsa, salt, pepper

UK: 2 large courgettis (sliced into rounds), 30ml olive oil, 100g shredded cheddar cheese, 1 jalapeño (sliced), 50g black beans, 2 tablespoons sour cream, 2 tablespoons salsa, salt, pepper

Instructions:

1. Preheat your Salter Air Fryer to 200°C (392°F).
2. Toss the zucchini slices with olive oil, salt, and pepper.
3. Arrange the slices in the air fryer basket in a single layer and cook for 8-10 minutes until slightly crispy.
4. Top with shredded cheddar, jalapeño slices, and black beans.

5. Cook for an additional 5 minutes until the cheese is melted.

6. Serve with a dollop of sour cream and salsa on top.

Nutritional Info: Calories: 180 Fat: 12g Carbs: 10g Protein: 8g

Turkey Meatballs

Prep: 15 mins Cook: 15 mins Serves: 4

Ingredients:

US: 500g ground turkey, 1 large egg, 50g breadcrumbs, 1 small onion (finely chopped), 2 cloves garlic (minced), 1 teaspoon dried oregano, salt, pepper, 30ml olive oil

UK: 500g ground turkey, 1 large egg, 50g breadcrumbs, 1 small onion (finely chopped), 2 cloves garlic (minced), 1 teaspoon dried oregano, salt, pepper, 30ml olive oil

Instructions:

1. Preheat your Salter Air Fryer to 200°C (392°F).

2. In a bowl, combine the ground turkey, egg, breadcrumbs, onion, garlic, oregano, salt, and pepper.

3. Shape the mixture into meatballs about the size of a golf ball.

4. Brush each meatball with a bit of olive oil and place in the air fryer basket.

5. Cook for 12-15 minutes, shaking the basket halfway through, until the meatballs are cooked through and golden.

6. Serve with your favourite dipping sauce or over pasta.

Nutritional Info: Calories: 250 Fat: 12g Carbs: 10g Protein: 25g

Eggplant Parmesan

Prep: 15 mins Cook: 20 mins Serves: 4

Ingredients:

US: 2 medium eggplants (sliced into rounds), 50g flour, 2 large eggs (beaten), 100g breadcrumbs, 50g grated Parmesan cheese, 50ml marinara sauce, 50g mozzarella cheese (shredded), salt, pepper, olive oil spray

UK: 2 medium auberges (sliced into rounds), 50g flour, 2 large eggs (beaten), 100g breadcrumbs, 50g grated Parmesan cheese, 50ml marinara sauce, 50g mozzarella cheese (shredded), salt, pepper, olive oil spray

Instructions:

1. Preheat your Salter Air Fryer to 200°C (392°F).
2. Set up a breading station with flour, beaten eggs, and breadcrumbs mixed with grated Parmesan, salt, and pepper.
3. Dip each eggplant slice in flour, then egg, and finally coat with breadcrumbs.
4. Arrange the breaded eggplant slices in the air fryer basket and spray lightly with olive oil.
5. Cook for 12-15 minutes, turning halfway through, until golden and crispy.
6. Top each slice with marinara sauce and shredded mozzarella, then cook for an additional 5 minutes until the cheese is melted.
7. Serve immediately with fresh basil, if desired.

Nutritional Info: Calories: 220 Fat: 10g Carbs: 20g Protein: 10g

Crispy Tofu Stir Fry

Prep: 10 mins Cook: 20 mins Serves: 4

Ingredients:

US: 400g firm tofu (cubed), 30ml soy sauce, 1 tablespoon cornstarch, 2 tablespoons olive oil, 1 red bell pepper (sliced), 1 yellow bell pepper (sliced), 100g snap peas, 2 cloves garlic (minced), 1 tablespoon ginger (grated), 30ml hoisin sauce

UK: 400g firm tofu (cubed), 30ml soy sauce, 1 tablespoon corn flour, 2 tablespoons olive oil, 1 red pepper (sliced), 1 yellow pepper (sliced), 100g mange tout, 2 cloves garlic (minced), 1 tablespoon ginger (grated), 30ml hoisin sauce

Instructions:

1. Preheat your Salter Air Fryer to 200°C (392°F).
2. Toss the tofu cubes with soy sauce and cornstarch until well coated.
3. Place the tofu in the air fryer basket and cook for 10 minutes, shaking the basket halfway through.
4. Heat olive oil in a pan and sauté the bell peppers, snap peas, garlic, and ginger for 5 minutes until tender.
5. Add the cooked tofu to the pan and stir in the hoisin sauce. Cook for another 2-3 minutes until everything is well coated.
6. Serve immediately over rice or noodles.

Nutritional Info: Calories: 250 Fat: 15g Carbs: 15g Protein: 15g

Buffalo Cauliflower Bites

Prep: 10 mins Cook: 15 mins Serves: 4

Ingredients:

US: 1 large head cauliflower (cut into florets), 30ml olive oil, 50g flour, 1 teaspoon garlic powder, 1 teaspoon onion powder, 50ml hot sauce, 30g butter (melted), salt, pepper

UK: 1 large head cauliflower (cut into florets), 30ml olive oil, 50g flour, 1 teaspoon garlic powder, 1 teaspoon onion powder, 50ml hot sauce, 30g butter (melted), salt, pepper

Instructions:

1. Preheat your Salter Air Fryer to 200°C (392°F).
2. In a bowl, toss the cauliflower florets with olive oil, flour, garlic powder, onion powder, salt, and pepper until well coated.
3. Place the cauliflower in the air fryer basket in a single layer and cook for 12-15 minutes, shaking the basket halfway through.
4. In a separate bowl, mix the hot sauce with melted butter.
5. Toss the cooked cauliflower in the hot sauce mixture until well-coated.
6. Serve immediately with a side of ranch or blue cheese dressing.

Nutritional Info: Calories: 150 Fat: 10g Carbs: 10g Protein: 5g

Portobello Mushroom Pizzas

Prep: 10 mins Cook: 15 mins Serves: 4

Ingredients:

US: 4 large portobello mushrooms (stems removed), 50ml marinara sauce, 100g mozzarella cheese (shredded), 50g pepperoni slices, 1 teaspoon dried oregano, olive oil spray, salt, pepper

UK: 4 large portobello mushrooms (stems removed), 50ml marinara sauce, 100g mozzarella cheese (shredded), 50g pepperoni slices, 1 teaspoon dried oregano, olive oil spray, salt, pepper

Instructions:

1. Preheat your Salter Air Fryer to 180°C (356°F).
2. Spray the mushrooms with olive oil and season with salt and pepper.
3. Place the mushrooms in the air fryer basket and cook for 5 minutes to soften.
4. Remove the mushrooms and top each with marinara sauce, shredded mozzarella, and pepperoni slices.
5. Return to the air fryer and cook for an additional 8-10 minutes until the cheese is melted and bubbly.
6. Sprinkle with dried oregano before serving.

Nutritional Info: Calories: 200 Fat: 15g Carbs: 5g Protein: 10g

Baked Falafel

Prep: 10 mins Cook: 15 mins Serves: 4

Ingredients:

US: 400g chickpeas (drained and rinsed), 1 small onion (finely chopped), 2 cloves garlic (minced), 1 teaspoon ground cumin, 1 teaspoon ground coriander, 1 teaspoon baking powder, 30g flour, 2 tablespoons olive oil, salt, pepper, fresh parsley (chopped)

UK: 400g chickpeas (drained and rinsed), 1 small onion (finely chopped), 2 cloves garlic (minced), 1 teaspoon ground cumin, 1 teaspoon ground coriander, 1 teaspoon baking powder, 30g flour, 2 tablespoons olive oil, salt, pepper, fresh parsley (chopped)

Instructions:

1. Preheat your Salter Air Fryer to 200°C (392°F).
2. In a food processor, combine chickpeas, onion, garlic, cumin, coriander, baking powder, flour, salt, and pepper until well-mixed but still slightly chunky.
3. Shape the mixture into small balls or patties.
4. Brush each falafel with olive oil and place in the air fryer basket.
5. Cook for 12-15 minutes, turning halfway through, until golden and crispy.
6. Serve immediately with a side of tahini sauce or in a pita with fresh vegetables.

Nutritional Info: Calories: 220 Fat: 10g Carbs: 25g Protein: 7g

Crispy Coconut Chicken

Prep: 15 mins Cook: 15 mins Serves: 4

Ingredients:

US: 500g chicken breasts (cut into strips), 50g flour, 2 large eggs (beaten), 100g desiccated coconut, 50g breadcrumbs, 30ml coconut milk, salt, pepper, sweet chilli sauce (for serving)

UK: 500g chicken breasts (cut into strips), 50g flour, 2 large eggs (beaten), 100g desiccated coconut, 50g breadcrumbs, 30ml coconut milk, salt, pepper, sweet chilli sauce (for serving)

Instructions:
1. Preheat your Salter Air Fryer to 200°C (392°F).
2. Set up a breading station with flour, beaten eggs mixed with coconut milk, and a mixture of desiccated coconut and breadcrumbs.
3. Season the chicken strips with salt and pepper.
4. Dip each chicken strip in flour, then egg mixture, and finally coat with the coconut and breadcrumb mixture.
5. Place the breaded chicken strips in the air fryer basket in a single layer.
6. Cook for 12-15 minutes, shaking the basket halfway through, until the chicken is golden and crispy.
7. Serve immediately with sweet chilli sauce for dipping.

Nutritional Info: Calories: 350 Fat: 15g Carbs: 25g Protein: 25g

Veggie Chips Medley

Prep: 10 mins Cook: 20 mins Serves: 4

Ingredients:
US: 1 large sweet potato (sliced thin), 2 large carrots (sliced thin), 1 large beetroot (sliced thin), 30ml olive oil, salt, pepper, paprika

UK: 1 large sweet potato (sliced thin), 2 large carrots (sliced thin), 1 large beetroot (sliced thin), 30ml olive oil, salt, pepper, paprika

Instructions:
1. Preheat your Salter Air Fryer to 180°C (356°F).
2. Toss the vegetable slices with olive oil, salt, pepper, and a sprinkle of paprika.
3. Place the slices in the air fryer basket in a single layer.
4. Cook for 15-20 minutes, shaking the basket halfway through, until the chips are crispy and golden.
5. Serve immediately as a healthy snack or side dish.

Nutritional Info: Calories: 150 Fat: 7g Carbs: 20g Protein: 2g

Sesame Crusted Tuna Steaks

Prep: 10 mins Cook: 8 mins Serves: 4

Ingredients:

US: 4 tuna steaks, 30ml soy sauce, 2 tablespoons sesame oil, 50g sesame seeds, salt, pepper, lemon wedges (for serving)

UK: 4 tuna steaks, 30ml soy sauce, 2 tablespoons sesame oil, 50g sesame seeds, salt, pepper, lemon wedges (for serving)

Instructions:

1. Preheat your Salter Air Fryer to 200°C (392°F).
2. Marinate the tuna steaks in soy sauce and sesame oil for 5 minutes.
3. Coat each steak with sesame seeds and season with salt and pepper.
4. Place the tuna steaks in the air fryer basket in a single layer.
5. Cook for 6-8 minutes, flipping halfway through, until the tuna is cooked to your desired level of doneness.
6. Serve immediately with lemon wedges.

Nutritional Info: Calories: 300 Fat: 15g Carbs: 5g Protein: 35g

Stuffed Bell Pepper Boats

Prep: 15 mins Cook: 20 mins Serves: 4

Ingredients:

US: 4 large bell peppers (halved and seeds removed), 250g ground turkey, 100g cooked quinoa, 1 small onion (finely chopped), 2 cloves garlic (minced), 50g shredded cheddar cheese, 1 teaspoon cumin, 1 teaspoon paprika, salt, pepper

UK: 4 large bell peppers (halved and seeds removed), 250g ground turkey, 100g cooked quinoa, 1 small onion (finely chopped), 2 cloves garlic (minced), 50g shredded cheddar cheese, 1 teaspoon cumin, 1 teaspoon paprika, salt, pepper

Instructions:

1. Preheat your Salter Air Fryer to 180°C (356°F).
2. In a pan, sauté the onion and garlic until soft. Add the ground turkey and cook until browned.
3. Stir in the cooked quinoa, cumin, paprika, salt, and pepper.
4. Fill each bell pepper half with the turkey mixture.
5. Place the stuffed peppers in the air fryer basket and cook for 15-20 minutes until the peppers are tender.
6. Sprinkle with shredded cheddar and cook for an additional 5 minutes until the cheese is melted.
7. Serve immediately.

Nutritional Info: Calories: 300 Fat: 12g Carbs: 20g Protein: 25g

CHAPTER 7: KID-FRIENDLY FARE (15 RECIPES)

Homemade Chicken Nuggets

Prep: 15 mins Cook: 10 mins Serves: 4

Ingredients:

US: 500g chicken breast (cut into bite-sized pieces), 50g flour, 2 eggs (beaten), 100g breadcrumbs, 1 teaspoon garlic powder, 1 teaspoon onion powder, salt, pepper, 1 tablespoon olive oil

UK: 500g chicken breast (cut into bite-sized pieces), 50g flour, 2 eggs (beaten), 100g breadcrumbs, 1 teaspoon garlic powder, 1 teaspoon onion powder, salt, pepper, 1 tablespoon olive oil

Instructions:

1. Preheat your Salter air fryer to 200°C (390°F).
2. Season the chicken pieces with garlic powder, onion powder, salt, and pepper.
3. Dredge each piece in flour, dip in beaten eggs, and coat with breadcrumbs.
4. Lightly brush the nuggets with olive oil and place them in the air fryer basket.
5. Cook for 10 minutes, turning halfway through, until golden and crispy.
6. Serve hot with your favourite dipping sauce.

Nutritional Info: Calories: 280 Fat: 10g Carbs: 20g Protein: 25g

Mini Pizzas

Prep: 10 mins Cook: 8 mins Serves: 4

Ingredients:

US: 4 small pizza bases, 200g pizza sauce, 200g mozzarella cheese (grated), 50g pepperoni slices, 50g bell peppers (chopped), 1 tablespoon olive oil, salt, pepper

UK: 4 small pizza bases, 200g pizza sauce, 200g mozzarella cheese (grated), 50g pepperoni slices, 50g bell peppers (chopped), 1 tablespoon olive oil, salt, pepper

Instructions:

1. Preheat your Salter air fryer to 200°C (390°F).
2. Spread pizza sauce evenly over each pizza base.
3. Top with grated mozzarella, pepperoni slices, and chopped bell peppers.
4. Lightly brush the edges with olive oil.
5. Place the pizzas in the air fryer basket and cook for 8 minutes, until the cheese is melted and bubbly.
6. Serve hot and enjoy your mini pizzas.

Nutritional Info: Calories: 350 Fat: 15g Carbs: 30g Protein: 20g

Crispy Fish Fingers

Prep: 15 mins Cook: 12 mins Serves: 4

Ingredients:

US: 400g white fish fillets (cut into strips), 50g flour, 2 eggs (beaten), 100g breadcrumbs, 1 teaspoon paprika, 1 tablespoon olive oil, salt, pepper

UK: 400g white fish fillets (cut into strips), 50g flour, 2 eggs (beaten), 100g breadcrumbs, 1 teaspoon paprika, 1 tablespoon olive oil, salt, pepper

Instructions:

1. Preheat your Salter air fryer to 190°C (375°F).
2. Season the fish strips with paprika, salt, and pepper.
3. Dredge each strip in flour, dip in beaten eggs, and coat with breadcrumbs.
4. Lightly brush the fish fingers with olive oil and place them in the air fryer basket.
5. Cook for 12 minutes, turning halfway through, until golden and crispy.
6. Serve hot with tartar sauce or ketchup.

Nutritional Info: Calories: 250 Fat: 8g Carbs: 20g Protein: 20g

Mac and Cheese Bites

Prep: 20 mins Cook: 10 mins Serves: 4

Ingredients:

US: 200g cooked macaroni, 100g cheddar cheese (grated), 50g Parmesan cheese (grated), 2 eggs (beaten), 100g breadcrumbs, 1 tablespoon olive oil, salt, pepper

UK: 200g cooked macaroni, 100g cheddar cheese (grated), 50g Parmesan cheese (grated), 2 eggs (beaten), 100g breadcrumbs, 1 tablespoon olive oil, salt, pepper

Instructions:

1. Preheat your Salter air fryer to 200°C (390°F).
2. In a bowl, mix the cooked macaroni with grated cheddar and Parmesan cheese, beaten eggs, salt, and pepper.
3. Form the mixture into small balls and coat with breadcrumbs.
4. Lightly brush the mac and cheese bites with olive oil and place them in the air fryer basket.
5. Cook for 10 minutes, turning halfway through, until golden and crispy.
6. Serve hot with marinara sauce or ranch dressing.

Nutritional Info: Calories: 300 Fat: 15g Carbs: 25g Protein: 15g

Sweet Potato Tots

Prep: 15 mins Cook: 15 mins Serves: 4

Ingredients:

US: 400g sweet potatoes (peeled and grated), 1 egg (beaten), 50g breadcrumbs, 1 teaspoon garlic powder, 1 teaspoon onion powder, 1 tablespoon olive oil, salt, pepper

UK: 400g sweet potatoes (peeled and grated), 1 egg (beaten), 50g breadcrumbs, 1 teaspoon garlic powder, 1 teaspoon onion powder, 1 tablespoon olive oil, salt, pepper

Instructions:

1. Preheat your Salter air fryer to 190°C (375°F).
2. In a bowl, mix the grated sweet potatoes with beaten egg, breadcrumbs, garlic powder, onion powder, salt, and pepper.
3. Form the mixture into small tots.
4. Lightly brush the tots with olive oil and place them in the air fryer basket.
5. Cook for 15 minutes, turning halfway through, until crispy and golden.
6. Serve hot with ketchup or your favourite dipping sauce.

Nutritional Info: Calories: 200 Fat: 8g Carbs: 30g Protein: 3g

Cheesy Broccoli Fritters

Prep: 15 mins Cook: 10 mins Serves: 4

Ingredients:

US: 300g broccoli (finely chopped), 100g cheddar cheese (grated), 1 egg (beaten), 50g flour, 1 tablespoon olive oil, salt, pepper

UK: 300g broccoli (finely chopped), 100g cheddar cheese (grated), 1 egg (beaten), 50g flour, 1 tablespoon olive oil, salt, pepper

Instructions:

1. Preheat your Salter air fryer to 180°C (350°F).
2. In a bowl, mix the chopped broccoli with grated cheddar cheese, beaten egg, flour, salt, and pepper.
3. Form the mixture into small patties.
4. Lightly brush the fritters with olive oil and place them in the air fryer basket.
5. Cook for 10 minutes, turning halfway through, until golden and crispy.
6. Serve hot with a dollop of sour cream.

Nutritional Info: Calories: 250 Fat: 12g Carbs: 15g Protein: 15g

Crispy Corn Dogs

Prep: 20 mins Cook: 10 mins Serves: 4

Ingredients:

US: 4 hot dogs, 100g cornmeal, 50g flour, 1 egg (beaten), 100ml milk, 1 teaspoon baking powder, 1 tablespoon olive oil, salt, pepper, 4 wooden skewers

UK: 4 hot dogs, 100g cornmeal, 50g flour, 1 egg (beaten), 100ml milk, 1 teaspoon baking powder, 1 tablespoon olive oil, salt, pepper, 4 wooden skewers

Instructions:

1. Preheat your Salter air fryer to 190°C (375°F).
2. Insert a wooden skewer into each hot dog.
3. In a bowl, mix the cornmeal, flour, beaten egg, milk, baking powder, salt, and pepper to make a thick batter.
4. Dip each hot dog into the batter, ensuring it is fully coated.
5. Lightly brush the corn dogs with olive oil and place them in the air fryer basket.
6. Cook for 10 minutes, turning halfway through, until golden and crispy.
7. Serve hot with mustard and ketchup.

Nutritional Info: Calories: 300 Fat: 15g Carbs: 30g Protein: 10g

Apple Cinnamon Chips

Prep: 10 mins Cook: 15 mins Serves: 4

Ingredients:

US: 3 apples (thinly sliced), 1 teaspoon cinnamon, 1 tablespoon sugar, 1 tablespoon olive oil
UK: 3 apples (thinly sliced), 1 teaspoon cinnamon, 1 tablespoon sugar, 1 tablespoon olive oil

Instructions:

1. Preheat your Salter air fryer to 180°C (350°F).
2. In a bowl, toss the apple slices with cinnamon, sugar, and olive oil.
3. Arrange the apple slices in a single layer in the air fryer basket.
4. Cook for 15 minutes, turning halfway through, until crispy.
5. Serve the apple cinnamon chips as a healthy snack.

Nutritional Info: Calories: 100 Fat: 3g Carbs: 20g Protein: 0g

Carrot Fries

Prep: 10 mins Cook: 15 mins Serves: 4

Ingredients:

US: 500g carrots (peeled and cut into sticks), 1 tablespoon olive oil, 1 teaspoon garlic powder, 1 teaspoon paprika, salt, pepper

UK: 500g carrots (peeled and cut into sticks), 1 tablespoon olive oil, 1 teaspoon garlic powder, 1 teaspoon paprika, salt, pepper

Instructions:

1. Preheat your Salter air fryer to 200°C (390°F).
2. In a bowl, toss the carrot sticks with olive oil, garlic powder, paprika, salt, and pepper.
3. Arrange the carrot sticks in a single layer in the air fryer basket.
4. Cook for 15 minutes, shaking the basket halfway through, until crispy and golden.
5. Serve the carrot fries hot as a tasty side dish.

Nutritional Info: Calories: 150 Fat: 5g Carbs: 25g Protein: 2g

Crispy Tofu Fingers

Prep: 15 mins Cook: 10 mins Serves: 4

Ingredients:

US: 400g firm tofu (cut into sticks), 50g corn flour, 2 tablespoons soy sauce, 1 teaspoon garlic powder, 1 teaspoon paprika, 1 tablespoon olive oil

UK: 400g firm tofu (cut into sticks), 50g corn flour, 2 tablespoons soy sauce, 1 teaspoon garlic powder, 1 teaspoon paprika, 1 tablespoon olive oil

Instructions:

1. Preheat your Salter air fryer to 200°C (390°F).
2. In a bowl, toss the tofu sticks with soy sauce, garlic powder, and paprika.
3. Dredge each tofu stick in corn flour.
4. Lightly brush the tofu fingers with olive oil and place them in the air fryer basket.
5. Cook for 10 minutes, turning halfway through, until golden and crispy.
6. Serve hot with a dipping sauce of your choice.

Nutritional Info: Calories: 200 Fat: 10g Carbs: 15g Protein: 10g

Zucchini Pizza Bites

Prep: 10 mins Cook: 8 mins Serves: 4

Ingredients:

US: 2 large zucchinis (sliced into rounds), 100g pizza sauce, 100g mozzarella cheese (grated), 50g pepperoni slices, 1 tablespoon olive oil, salt, pepper

UK: 2 large zucchinis (sliced into rounds), 100g pizza sauce, 100g mozzarella cheese (grated), 50g pepperoni slices, 1 tablespoon olive oil, salt, pepper

Instructions:

1. Preheat your Salter air fryer to 200°C (390°F).
2. Arrange the zucchini rounds in a single layer in the air fryer basket.
3. Top each round with a small amount of pizza sauce, grated mozzarella, and a slice of pepperoni.
4. Lightly brush the zucchini bites with olive oil.
5. Cook for 8 minutes, until the cheese is melted and bubbly.
6. Serve the zucchini pizza bites hot as a low-carb snack.

Nutritional Info: Calories: 100 Fat: 7g Carbs: 5g Protein: 5g

Peanut Butter Banana Roll-Ups

Prep: 10 mins Cook: 5 mins Serves: 4

Ingredients:

US: 4 tortillas, 2 bananas (sliced), 4 tablespoons peanut butter, 1 tablespoon honey, 1 tablespoon olive oil

UK: 4 tortillas, 2 bananas (sliced), 4 tablespoons peanut butter, 1 tablespoon honey, 1 tablespoon olive oil

Instructions:

1. Preheat your Salter air fryer to 180°C (350°F).
2. Spread peanut butter evenly over each tortilla.
3. Place banana slices on one side of each tortilla and drizzle with honey.
4. Roll up the tortillas tightly.
5. Lightly brush the roll-ups with olive oil and place them in the air fryer basket.
6. Cook for 5 minutes, until golden and crispy.
7. Serve the peanut butter banana roll-ups warm as a sweet treat.

Nutritional Info: Calories: 250 Fat: 12g Carbs: 30g Protein: 5g

Crispy Chicken Sliders

Prep: 20 mins Cook: 10 mins Serves: 4

Ingredients:

US: 4 small chicken breasts (pounded thin), 50g flour, 2 eggs (beaten), 100g breadcrumbs, 1 teaspoon paprika, 1 tablespoon olive oil, 4 small buns, lettuce, tomato slices, mayonnaise, salt, pepper

UK: 4 small chicken breasts (pounded thin), 50g flour, 2 eggs (beaten), 100g breadcrumbs, 1 teaspoon paprika, 1 tablespoon olive oil, 4 small buns, lettuce, tomato slices, mayonnaise, salt, pepper

Instructions:

1. Preheat your Salter air fryer to 200°C (390°F).
2. Season the chicken breasts with paprika, salt, and pepper.
3. Dredge each breast in flour, dip in beaten eggs, and coat with breadcrumbs.
4. Lightly brush the chicken with olive oil and place it in the air fryer basket.
5. Cook for 10 minutes, turning halfway through, until golden and crispy.
6. Assemble the sliders by placing the cooked chicken on buns with lettuce, tomato slices, and mayonnaise.
7. Serve the crispy chicken sliders hot.

Nutritional Info: Calories: 350 Fat: 15g Carbs: 30g Protein: 20g

Cauliflower Popcorn

Prep: 10 mins Cook: 15 mins Serves: 4

Ingredients:

US: 1 large cauliflower (cut into small florets), 50g flour, 1 teaspoon garlic powder, 1 teaspoon paprika, 1 tablespoon olive oil, salt, pepper
UK: 1 large cauliflower (cut into small florets), 50g flour, 1 teaspoon garlic powder, 1 teaspoon paprika, 1 tablespoon olive oil, salt, pepper

Instructions:

1. Preheat your Salter air fryer to 200°C (390°F).
2. In a bowl, toss the cauliflower florets with flour, garlic powder, paprika, salt, and pepper.

3. Lightly brush the cauliflower with olive oil and place it in the air fryer basket.

4. Cook for 15 minutes, shaking the basket halfway through, until golden and crispy.

5. Serve the cauliflower popcorn hot as a healthy snack.

Nutritional Info: Calories: 100 Fat: 5g Carbs: 15g Protein: 3g

Cinnamon Sugar Donut Holes

Prep: 15 mins Cook: 8 mins Serves: 4

Ingredients:

US: 200g flour, 50g sugar, 1 teaspoon baking powder, 1/2 teaspoon cinnamon, 1/4 teaspoon nutmeg, 1 egg (beaten), 100ml milk, 1 tablespoon olive oil, 50g sugar, 1 teaspoon cinnamon

UK: 200g flour, 50g sugar, 1 teaspoon baking powder, 1/2 teaspoon cinnamon, 1/4 teaspoon nutmeg, 1 egg (beaten), 100ml milk, 1 tablespoon olive oil, 50g sugar, 1 teaspoon cinnamon

Instructions:

1. Preheat your Salter air fryer to 180°C (350°F).

2. In a bowl, mix flour, sugar, baking powder, cinnamon, and nutmeg.

3. Add beaten egg and milk, stirring until a dough forms.

4. Form the dough into small balls.

5. Lightly brush the doughnut holes with olive oil and place them in the air fryer basket.

6. Cook for 8 minutes, shaking the basket halfway through, until golden and cooked through.

7. In a separate bowl, mix 50g sugar and 1 teaspoon cinnamon.

8. Roll the cooked doughnut holes in the cinnamon sugar mixture.

9. Serve the cinnamon sugar doughnut holes warm.

Nutritional Info: Calories: 200 Fat: 8g Carbs: 30g Protein: 3g

CHAPTER 8: PARTY PLEASERS (15 RECIPES)

Homemade Chicken Nuggets

Prep: 15 mins Cook: 10 mins Serves: 4

Ingredients:

US: 500g chicken breast (cut into bite-sized pieces), 50g flour, 2 eggs (beaten), 100g breadcrumbs, 1 teaspoon garlic powder, 1 teaspoon onion powder, salt, pepper, 1 tablespoon olive oil

UK: 500g chicken breast (cut into bite-sized pieces), 50g flour, 2 eggs (beaten), 100g breadcrumbs, 1 teaspoon garlic powder, 1 teaspoon onion powder, salt, pepper, 1 tablespoon olive oil

Instructions:

1. Preheat your Salter air fryer to 200°C (390°F).
2. Season the chicken pieces with garlic powder, onion powder, salt, and pepper.
3. Dredge each piece in flour, dip in beaten eggs, and coat with breadcrumbs.
4. Lightly brush the nuggets with olive oil and place them in the air fryer basket.
5. Cook for 10 minutes, turning halfway through, until golden and crispy.
6. Serve hot with your favourite dipping sauce.

Nutritional Info: Calories: 280 Fat: 10g Carbs: 20g Protein: 25g

Mini Pizzas

Prep: 10 mins Cook: 8 mins Serves: 4

Ingredients:

US: 4 small pizza bases, 200g pizza sauce, 200g mozzarella cheese (grated), 50g pepperoni slices, 50g bell peppers (chopped), 1 tablespoon olive oil, salt, pepper

UK: 4 small pizza bases, 200g pizza sauce, 200g mozzarella cheese (grated), 50g pepperoni slices, 50g bell peppers (chopped), 1 tablespoon olive oil, salt, pepper

Instructions:

1. Preheat your Salter air fryer to 200°C (390°F).
2. Spread pizza sauce evenly over each pizza base.
3. Top with grated mozzarella, pepperoni slices, and chopped bell peppers.
4. Lightly brush the edges with olive oil.
5. Place the pizzas in the air fryer basket and cook for 8 minutes, until the cheese is melted and bubbly.
6. Serve hot and enjoy your mini pizzas.

Nutritional Info: Calories: 350 Fat: 15g Carbs: 30g Protein: 20g

Crispy Fish Fingers

Prep: 15 mins Cook: 12 mins Serves: 4

Ingredients:

US: 400g white fish fillets (cut into strips), 50g flour, 2 eggs (beaten), 100g breadcrumbs, 1 teaspoon paprika, 1 tablespoon olive oil, salt, pepper

UK: 400g white fish fillets (cut into strips), 50g flour, 2 eggs (beaten), 100g breadcrumbs, 1 teaspoon paprika, 1 tablespoon olive oil, salt, pepper

Instructions:

1. Preheat your Salter air fryer to 190°C (375°F).
2. Season the fish strips with paprika, salt, and pepper.
3. Dredge each strip in flour, dip in beaten eggs, and coat with breadcrumbs.
4. Lightly brush the fish fingers with olive oil and place them in the air fryer basket.
5. Cook for 12 minutes, turning halfway through, until golden and crispy.
6. Serve hot with tartar sauce or ketchup.

Nutritional Info: Calories: 250 Fat: 8g Carbs: 20g Protein: 20g

Mac and Cheese Bites

Prep: 20 mins Cook: 10 mins Serves: 4

Ingredients:

US: 200g cooked macaroni, 100g cheddar cheese (grated), 50g Parmesan cheese (grated), 2 eggs (beaten), 100g breadcrumbs, 1 tablespoon olive oil, salt, pepper

UK: 200g cooked macaroni, 100g cheddar cheese (grated), 50g Parmesan cheese (grated), 2 eggs (beaten), 100g breadcrumbs, 1 tablespoon olive oil, salt, pepper

Instructions:

1. Preheat your Salter air fryer to 200°C (390°F).
2. In a bowl, mix the cooked macaroni with grated cheddar and Parmesan cheese, beaten eggs, salt, and pepper.
3. Form the mixture into small balls and coat with breadcrumbs.
4. Lightly brush the mac and cheese bites with olive oil and place them in the air fryer basket.
5. Cook for 10 minutes, turning halfway through, until golden and crispy.
6. Serve hot with marinara sauce or ranch dressing.

Nutritional Info: Calories: 300 Fat: 15g Carbs: 25g Protein: 15g

Sweet Potato Tots

Prep: 15 mins Cook: 15 mins Serves: 4

Ingredients:

US: 400g sweet potatoes (peeled and grated), 1 egg (beaten), 50g breadcrumbs, 1 teaspoon garlic powder, 1 teaspoon onion powder, 1 tablespoon olive oil, salt, pepper

UK: 400g sweet potatoes (peeled and grated), 1 egg (beaten), 50g breadcrumbs, 1 teaspoon garlic powder, 1 teaspoon onion powder, 1 tablespoon olive oil, salt, pepper

Instructions:

1. Preheat your Salter air fryer to 190°C (375°F).
2. In a bowl, mix the grated sweet potatoes with beaten egg, breadcrumbs, garlic powder, onion powder, salt, and pepper.
3. Form the mixture into small tots.
4. Lightly brush the tots with olive oil and place them in the air fryer basket.
5. Cook for 15 minutes, turning halfway through, until crispy and golden.
6. Serve hot with ketchup or your favourite dipping sauce.

Nutritional Info: Calories: 200 Fat: 8g Carbs: 30g Protein: 3g

Cheesy Broccoli Fritters

Prep: 15 mins Cook: 10 mins Serves: 4

Ingredients:

US: 300g broccoli (finely chopped), 100g cheddar cheese (grated), 1 egg (beaten), 50g flour, 1 tablespoon olive oil, salt, pepper

UK: 300g broccoli (finely chopped), 100g cheddar cheese (grated), 1 egg (beaten), 50g flour, 1 tablespoon olive oil, salt, pepper

Instructions:

1. Preheat your Salter air fryer to 180°C (350°F).
2. In a bowl, mix the chopped broccoli with grated cheddar cheese, beaten egg, flour, salt, and pepper.
3. Form the mixture into small patties.
4. Lightly brush the fritters with olive oil and place them in the air fryer basket.
5. Cook for 10 minutes, turning halfway through, until golden and crispy.
6. Serve hot with a dollop of sour cream.

Nutritional Info: Calories: 250 Fat: 12g Carbs: 15g Protein: 15g

Crispy Corn Dogs

Prep: 20 mins Cook: 10 mins Serves: 4

Ingredients:

US: 4 hot dogs, 100g cornmeal, 50g flour, 1 egg (beaten), 100ml milk, 1 teaspoon baking powder, 1 tablespoon olive oil, salt, pepper, 4 wooden skewers

UK: 4 hot dogs, 100g cornmeal, 50g flour, 1 egg (beaten), 100ml milk, 1 teaspoon baking powder, 1 tablespoon olive oil, salt, pepper, 4 wooden skewers

Instructions:

1. Preheat your Salter air fryer to 190°C (375°F).
2. Insert a wooden skewer into each hot dog.
3. In a bowl, mix the cornmeal, flour, beaten egg, milk, baking powder, salt, and pepper to make a thick batter.
4. Dip each hot dog into the batter, ensuring it is fully coated.
5. Lightly brush the corn dogs with olive oil and place them in the air fryer basket.
6. Cook for 10 minutes, turning halfway through, until golden and crispy.
7. Serve hot with mustard and ketchup.

Nutritional Info: Calories: 300 Fat: 15g Carbs: 30g Protein: 10g

Apple Cinnamon Chips

Prep: 10 mins Cook: 15 mins Serves: 4

Ingredients:

US: 3 apples (thinly sliced), 1 teaspoon cinnamon, 1 tablespoon sugar, 1 tablespoon olive oil
UK: 3 apples (thinly sliced), 1 teaspoon cinnamon, 1 tablespoon sugar, 1 tablespoon olive oil

Instructions:

1. Preheat your Salter air fryer to 180°C (350°F).
2. In a bowl, toss the apple slices with cinnamon, sugar, and olive oil.
3. Arrange the apple slices in a single layer in the air fryer basket.
4. Cook for 15 minutes, turning halfway through, until crispy.
5. Serve the apple cinnamon chips as a healthy snack.

Nutritional Info: Calories: 100 Fat: 3g Carbs: 20g Protein: 0g

Carrot Fries

Prep: 10 mins Cook: 15 mins Serves: 4

Ingredients:

US: 500g carrots (peeled and cut into sticks), 1 tablespoon olive oil, 1 teaspoon garlic powder, 1 teaspoon paprika, salt, pepper

UK: 500g carrots (peeled and cut into sticks), 1 tablespoon olive oil, 1 teaspoon garlic powder, 1 teaspoon paprika, salt, pepper

Instructions:

1. Preheat your Salter air fryer to 200°C (390°F).
2. In a bowl, toss the carrot sticks with olive oil, garlic powder, paprika, salt, and pepper.
3. Arrange the carrot sticks in a single layer in the air fryer basket.
4. Cook for 15 minutes, shaking the basket halfway through, until crispy and golden.
5. Serve the carrot fries hot as a tasty side dish.

Nutritional Info: Calories: 150 Fat: 5g Carbs: 25g Protein: 2g

Crispy Tofu Fingers

Prep: 15 mins Cook: 10 mins Serves: 4

Ingredients:

US: 400g firm tofu (cut into sticks), 50g corn flour, 2 tablespoons soy sauce, 1 teaspoon garlic powder, 1 teaspoon paprika, 1 tablespoon olive oil

UK: 400g firm tofu (cut into sticks), 50g corn flour, 2 tablespoons soy sauce, 1 teaspoon garlic powder, 1 teaspoon paprika, 1 tablespoon olive oil

Instructions:

1. Preheat your Salter air fryer to 200°C (390°F).
2. In a bowl, toss the tofu sticks with soy sauce, garlic powder, and paprika.
3. Dredge each tofu stick in corn flour.
4. Lightly brush the tofu fingers with olive oil and place them in the air fryer basket.
5. Cook for 10 minutes, turning halfway through, until golden and crispy.
6. Serve hot with a dipping sauce of your choice.

Nutritional Info: Calories: 200 Fat: 10g Carbs: 15g Protein: 10g

Zucchini Pizza Bites

Prep: 10 mins Cook: 8 mins Serves: 4

Ingredients:

US: 2 large zucchinis (sliced into rounds), 100g pizza sauce, 100g mozzarella cheese (grated), 50g pepperoni slices, 1 tablespoon olive oil, salt, pepper

UK: 2 large zucchinis (sliced into rounds), 100g pizza sauce, 100g mozzarella cheese (grated), 50g pepperoni slices, 1 tablespoon olive oil, salt, pepper

Instructions:

1. Preheat your Salter air fryer to 200°C (390°F).
2. Arrange the zucchini rounds in a single layer in the air fryer basket.
3. Top each round with a small amount of pizza sauce, grated mozzarella, and a slice of pepperoni.
4. Lightly brush the zucchini bites with olive oil.
5. Cook for 8 minutes, until the cheese is melted and bubbly.
6. Serve the zucchini pizza bites hot as a low-carb snack.

Nutritional Info: Calories: 100 Fat: 7g Carbs: 5g Protein: 5g

Peanut Butter Banana Roll-Ups

Prep: 10 mins Cook: 5 mins Serves: 4

Ingredients:

US: 4 tortillas, 2 bananas (sliced), 4 tablespoons peanut butter, 1 tablespoon honey, 1 tablespoon olive oil

UK: 4 tortillas, 2 bananas (sliced), 4 tablespoons peanut butter, 1 tablespoon honey, 1 tablespoon olive oil

Instructions:

1. Preheat your Salter air fryer to 180°C (350°F).
2. Spread peanut butter evenly over each tortilla.
3. Place banana slices on one side of each tortilla and drizzle with honey.
4. Roll up the tortillas tightly.
5. Lightly brush the roll-ups with olive oil and place them in the air fryer basket.
6. Cook for 5 minutes, until golden and crispy.
7. Serve the peanut butter banana roll-ups warm as a sweet treat.

Nutritional Info: Calories: 250 Fat: 12g Carbs: 30g Protein: 5g

Crispy Chicken Sliders

Prep: 20 mins Cook: 10 mins Serves: 4

Ingredients:

US: 4 small chicken breasts (pounded thin), 50g flour, 2 eggs (beaten), 100g breadcrumbs, 1 teaspoon paprika, 1 tablespoon olive oil, 4 small buns, lettuce, tomato slices, mayonnaise, salt, pepper

UK: 4 small chicken breasts (pounded thin), 50g flour, 2 eggs (beaten), 100g breadcrumbs, 1 teaspoon paprika, 1 tablespoon olive oil, 4 small buns, lettuce, tomato slices, mayonnaise, salt, pepper

Instructions:

1. Preheat your Salter air fryer to 200°C (390°F).
2. Season the chicken breasts with paprika, salt, and pepper.
3. Dredge each breast in flour, dip in beaten eggs, and coat with breadcrumbs.
4. Lightly brush the chicken with olive oil and place it in the air fryer basket.
5. Cook for 10 minutes, turning halfway through, until golden and crispy.
6. Assemble the sliders by placing the cooked chicken on buns with lettuce, tomato slices, and mayonnaise.
7. Serve the crispy chicken sliders hot.

Nutritional Info: Calories: 350 Fat: 15g Carbs: 30g Protein: 20g

Cauliflower Popcorn

Prep: 10 mins Cook: 15 mins Serves: 4

Ingredients:

US: 1 large cauliflower (cut into small florets), 50g flour, 1 teaspoon garlic powder, 1 teaspoon paprika, 1 tablespoon olive oil, salt, pepper

UK: 1 large cauliflower (cut into small florets), 50g flour, 1 teaspoon garlic powder, 1 teaspoon paprika, 1 tablespoon olive oil, salt, pepper

Instructions:

1. Preheat your Salter air fryer to 200°C (390°F).
2. In a bowl, toss the cauliflower florets with flour, garlic powder, paprika, salt, and pepper.
3. Lightly brush the cauliflower with olive oil and place it in the air fryer basket.
4. Cook for 15 minutes, shaking the basket halfway through, until golden and crispy.
5. Serve the cauliflower popcorn hot as a healthy snack.

Nutritional Info: Calories: 100 Fat: 5g Carbs: 15g Protein: 3g

Cinnamon Sugar Donut Holes

Prep: 15 mins Cook: 8 mins Serves: 4

Ingredients:

US: 200g flour, 50g sugar, 1 teaspoon baking powder, 1/2 teaspoon cinnamon, 1/4 teaspoon nutmeg, 1 egg (beaten), 100ml milk, 1 tablespoon olive oil, 50g sugar, 1 teaspoon cinnamon

UK: 200g flour, 50g sugar, 1 teaspoon baking powder, 1/2 teaspoon cinnamon, 1/4 teaspoon nutmeg, 1 egg (beaten), 100ml milk, 1 tablespoon olive oil, 50g sugar, 1 teaspoon cinnamon

Instructions:

1. Preheat your Salter air fryer to 180°C (350°F).
2. In a bowl, mix flour, sugar, baking powder, cinnamon, and nutmeg.
3. Add beaten egg and milk, stirring until a dough forms.
4. Form the dough into small balls.
5. Lightly brush the doughnut holes with olive oil and place them in the air fryer basket.
6. Cook for 8 minutes, shaking the basket halfway through, until golden and cooked through.
7. In a separate bowl, mix 50g sugar and 1 teaspoon cinnamon.
8. Roll the cooked doughnut holes in the cinnamon sugar mixture.
9. Serve the cinnamon sugar doughnut holes warm.

Nutritional Info: Calories: 200 Fat: 8g Carbs: 30g Protein: 3g

CHAPTER 9: SWEET TREATS

Apple Fritters

Prep: 15 mins Cook: 10 mins Serves: 4

Ingredients:
US: 2 apples (peeled and diced), 150g flour, 50g sugar, 1 teaspoon baking powder, 1/2 teaspoon cinnamon, 1/4 teaspoon nutmeg, 1 egg (beaten), 100ml milk, 1 tablespoon olive oil

UK: 2 apples (peeled and diced), 150g flour, 50g sugar, 1 teaspoon baking powder, 1/2 teaspoon cinnamon, 1/4 teaspoon nutmeg, 1 egg (beaten), 100ml milk, 1 tablespoon olive oil

Instructions:
1. Preheat your Salter air fryer to 180°C (350°F).
2. In a bowl, mix flour, sugar, baking powder, cinnamon, and nutmeg.
3. Add beaten egg and milk, stirring until a thick batter forms.
4. Fold in the diced apples.
5. Lightly brush the air fryer basket with olive oil.
6. Drop a spoonful of batter into the basket, spacing them apart.
7. Cook for 10 minutes, turning halfway through, until golden and crispy.
8. Serve the apple fritters warm, sprinkled with a bit of extra sugar.

Nutritional Info: Calories: 250 Fat: 8g Carbs: 40g Protein: 4g

Chocolate Lava Cakes

Prep: 15 mins Cook: 8 mins Serves: 4

Ingredients:
US: 150g dark chocolate (chopped), 100g butter, 100g sugar, 2 eggs, 50g flour, 1 teaspoon vanilla extract

UK: 150g dark chocolate (chopped), 100g butter, 100g sugar, 2 eggs, 50g flour, 1 teaspoon vanilla extract

Instructions:
1. Preheat your Salter air fryer to 200°C (390°F).
2. Melt the chocolate and butter together, stirring until smooth.
3. In a separate bowl, whisk together sugar and eggs until light and fluffy.
4. Gradually add the melted chocolate mixture and vanilla extract.
5. Fold in the flour until just combined.
6. Divide the batter between greased ramekins.

7. Place the ramekins in the air fryer basket and cook for 8 minutes.

8. Let the cakes cool for a minute before inverting onto plates.

9. Serve immediately to enjoy the gooey chocolate centre.

Nutritional Info: Calories: 400 Fat: 25g Carbs: 40g Protein: 6g

Cinnamon Sugar Churros

Prep: 10 mins Cook: 15 mins Serves: 4

Ingredients:

US: 100g flour, 100ml water, 50g butter, 1 tablespoon sugar, 1/4 teaspoon salt, 1/2 teaspoon vanilla extract, 1 tablespoon olive oil, 50g sugar, 1 teaspoon cinnamon

UK: 100g flour, 100ml water, 50g butter, 1 tablespoon sugar, 1/4 teaspoon salt, 1/2 teaspoon vanilla extract, 1 tablespoon olive oil, 50g sugar, 1 teaspoon cinnamon

Instructions:

1. Preheat your Salter air fryer to 200°C (390°F).

2. In a saucepan, bring water, butter, sugar, and salt to a boil.

3. Remove from heat and stir in flour until a dough forms.

4. Add vanilla extract and mix well.

5. Transfer the dough to a piping bag with a star tip.

6. Pipe strips of dough directly into the air fryer basket.

7. Lightly brush the churros with olive oil.

8. Cook for 10-15 minutes, turning halfway through, until golden and crispy.

9. In a bowl, mix sugar and cinnamon.

10. Toss the cooked churros in the cinnamon sugar mixture.

11. Serve warm with chocolate sauce for dipping.

Nutritional Info: Calories: 300 Fat: 12g Carbs: 45g Protein: 4g

Berry Crumble

Prep: 10 mins Cook: 15 mins Serves: 4

Ingredients:

US: 300g mixed berries, 50g sugar, 1 tablespoon lemon juice, 100g flour, 50g rolled oats, 50g brown sugar, 50g butter, 1/2 teaspoon cinnamon

UK: 300g mixed berries, 50g sugar, 1 tablespoon lemon juice, 100g flour, 50g rolled oats, 50g brown sugar, 50g butter, 1/2 teaspoon cinnamon

Instructions:

1. Preheat your Salter air fryer to 180°C (350°F).
2. In a bowl, toss the berries with sugar and lemon juice.
3. In another bowl, mix flour, oats, brown sugar, and cinnamon.
4. Cut in the butter until the mixture resembles coarse crumbs.
5. Divide the berries among small ramekins.
6. Sprinkle the crumble topping over the berries.
7. Place the ramekins in the air fryer basket and cook for 15 minutes.
8. Serve the berry crumble warm with a scoop of vanilla ice cream.

Nutritional Info: Calories: 250 Fat: 12g Carbs: 35g Protein: 3g

Banana Bread

Prep: 10 mins Cook: 25 mins Serves: 1 loaf

Ingredients:

US: 200g flour, 100g sugar, 1 teaspoon baking powder, 1/2 teaspoon baking soda, 1/4 teaspoon salt, 2 ripe bananas (mashed), 100ml milk, 1 egg, 50g butter (melted), 1 teaspoon vanilla extract

UK: 200g flour, 100g sugar, 1 teaspoon baking powder, 1/2 teaspoon baking soda, 1/4 teaspoon salt, 2 ripe bananas (mashed), 100ml milk, 1 egg, 50g butter (melted), 1 teaspoon vanilla extract

Instructions:

1. Preheat your Salter air fryer to 160°C (320°F).
2. In a bowl, mix flour, sugar, baking powder, baking soda, and salt.
3. In another bowl, combine mashed bananas, milk, egg, melted butter, and vanilla extract.
4. Add the wet ingredients to the dry ingredients and stir until just combined.
5. Pour the batter into a greased loaf pan.
6. Place the loaf pans in the air fryer basket and cook for 25 minutes, or until a toothpick inserted into the centre comes out clean.
7. Allow the banana bread to cool before slicing.
8. Serve warm or at room temperature.

Nutritional Info: Calories: 300 Fat: 10g Carbs: 45g Protein: 5g

Mini Cheesecakes

Prep: 15 mins Cook: 12 mins Serves: 6

Ingredients:

US: 100g digestive biscuits (crushed), 50g butter (melted), 200g cream cheese, 100g sugar, 1 egg, 1 teaspoon vanilla extract, 50ml sour cream

UK: 100g digestive biscuits (crushed), 50g butter (melted), 200g cream cheese, 100g sugar, 1 egg, 1 teaspoon vanilla extract, 50ml sour cream

Instructions:

1. Preheat your Salter air fryer to 160°C (320°F).
2. Mix crushed biscuits with melted butter and press into the bottom of 6 silicone muffin cups.
3. In a bowl, beat cream cheese and sugar until smooth.
4. Add egg, vanilla extract, and sour cream, mixing until well combined.
5. Pour the cheesecake mixture over the biscuit bases.
6. Place the muffin cups in the air fryer basket and cook for 12 minutes.
7. Allow the cheesecakes to cool, then refrigerate for at least 2 hours.
8. Serve the mini cheesecakes chilled, topped with fresh berries or fruit compote.

Nutritional Info: Calories: 200 Fat: 15g Carbs: 20g Protein: 3g

Peach Cobbler

Prep: 15 mins Cook: 20 mins Serves: 4

Ingredients:

US: 400g peaches (sliced), 50g sugar, 1 tablespoon lemon juice, 100g flour, 50g sugar, 1 teaspoon baking powder, 1/4 teaspoon salt, 50g butter (cold), 50ml milk

UK: 400g peaches (sliced), 50g sugar, 1 tablespoon lemon juice, 100g flour, 50g sugar, 1 teaspoon baking powder, 1/4 teaspoon salt, 50g butter (cold), 50ml milk

Instructions:

1. Preheat your Salter air fryer to 180°C (350°F).
2. In a bowl, toss the peach slices with sugar and lemon juice.
3. In another bowl, mix flour, sugar, baking powder, and salt.
4. Cut in the cold butter until the mixture resembles coarse crumbs.
5. Add milk and stir until just combined.
6. Pour the peaches into a greased baking dish.
7. Drop spoonful of the batter over the peaches.
8. Place the dish in the air fryer basket and cook for 20 minutes, until the topping is golden brown.

9. Serve the peach cobbler warm with a scoop of vanilla ice cream.

Nutritional Info: Calories: 300 Fat: 12g Carbs: 45g Protein: 3g

Peanut Butter Cookies

Prep: 10 mins Cook: 8 mins Serves: 12

Ingredients:

US: 200g peanut butter, 100g sugar, 1 egg, 1/2 teaspoon baking soda, 1/4 teaspoon salt

UK: 200g peanut butter, 100g sugar, 1 egg, 1/2 teaspoon baking soda, 1/4 teaspoon salt

Instructions:

1. Preheat your Salter air fryer to 180°C (350°F).
2. In a bowl, mix peanut butter, sugar, egg, baking soda, and salt until well combined.
3. Roll the dough into small balls and place them in the air fryer basket.
4. Flatten each ball with a fork, making a crisscross pattern.
5. Cook for 8 minutes, until the edges are golden.
6. Allow the cookies to cool before serving.

Nutritional Info: Calories: 150 Fat: 10g Carbs: 10g Protein: 5g

Crispy Cinnamon Rolls

Prep: 15 mins Cook: 12 mins Serves: 8

Ingredients:

US: 1 pack of pre-made cinnamon roll dough, 50g sugar, 1 teaspoon cinnamon, 1 tablespoon butter (melted)

UK: 1 pack of pre-made cinnamon roll dough, 50g sugar, 1 teaspoon cinnamon, 1 tablespoon butter (melted)

Instructions:

1. Preheat your Salter air fryer to 180°C (350°F).
2. In a bowl, mix sugar and cinnamon.
3. Brush the pre-made cinnamon roll dough with melted butter.
4. Sprinkle the cinnamon sugar mixture evenly over the dough.
5. Roll up the dough and cut into 8 equal pieces.
6. Place the rolls in the air fryer basket, spacing them apart.
7. Cook for 12 minutes, until golden and crispy.
8. Serve the crispy cinnamon rolls warm, optionally drizzled with icing.

Nutritional Info: Calories: 200 Fat: 8g Carbs: 30g Protein: 3g

Baked Apples

Prep: 10 mins Cook: 15 mins Serves: 4

Ingredients:

US: 4 apples (cored), 50g rolled oats, 30g brown sugar, 1 teaspoon cinnamon, 1/4 teaspoon nutmeg, 30g butter (melted)

UK: 4 apples (cored), 50g rolled oats, 30g brown sugar, 1 teaspoon cinnamon, 1/4 teaspoon nutmeg, 30g butter (melted)

Instructions:

1. Preheat your Salter air fryer to 180°C (350°F).
2. In a bowl, mix oats, brown sugar, cinnamon, nutmeg, and melted butter.
3. Stuff the mixture into the cored apples.
4. Place the apples in the air fryer basket.
5. Cook for 15 minutes, until the apples are tender.
6. Serve the baked apples warm, optionally with a scoop of vanilla ice cream.

Nutritional Info: Calories: 150 Fat: 5g Carbs: 25g Protein: 1g

Chocolate Chip Cookie Cups

Prep: 15 mins Cook: 10 mins Serves: 4

Ingredients:

US: 200g flour, 100g butter (softened), 100g sugar, 50g brown sugar, 1 egg, 1 teaspoon vanilla extract, 1/2 teaspoon baking soda, 100g chocolate chips

UK: 200g flour, 100g butter (softened), 100g sugar, 50g brown sugar, 1 egg, 1 teaspoon vanilla extract, 1/2 teaspoon baking soda, 100g chocolate chips

Instructions:

1. Preheat your Salter air fryer to 180°C (350°F).
2. In a bowl, cream together butter, sugar, and brown sugar until light and fluffy.
3. Beat in the egg and vanilla extract.
4. Add flour and baking soda, mixing until just combined.
5. Fold in the chocolate chips.
6. Divide the dough into greased muffin cups, pressing it down to form a cup shape.
7. Place the muffin cups in the air fryer basket and cook for 10 minutes, until golden.
8. Let the cookie cups cool before removing them from the muffin cups.
9. Serve the chocolate chip cookie cups with a scoop of ice cream.

Nutritional Info: Calories: 300 Fat: 15g Carbs: 40g Protein: 3g

Blueberry Muffins

Prep: 10 mins | Cook: 15 mins | Serves: 6

Ingredients:

US: 150g all-purpose flour, 100g granulated sugar, 1 teaspoon baking powder, 1/4 teaspoon salt, 1 egg, 120ml milk, 60ml vegetable oil, 100g fresh blueberries UK: 150g plain flour, 100g granulated sugar, 1 teaspoon baking powder, 1/4 teaspoon salt, 1 egg, 120ml milk, 60ml vegetable oil, 100g fresh blueberries

Instructions:

1. Preheat your Salter Air Fryer to 180°C (356°F).
2. In a bowl, mix flour, sugar, baking powder, and salt.
3. In another bowl, whisk together egg, milk, and vegetable oil.
4. Pour the wet ingredients into the dry ingredients and mix until just combined.
5. Gently fold in the blueberries.
6. Divide the batter among six muffin cups.
7. Place the muffin cups in the air fryer basket and cook for 12-15 minutes until a toothpick inserted into the centre comes out clean.
8. Let cool before serving.

Nutritional Info: Calories: 180 | Fat: 8g | Carbs: 25g | Protein: 3g

Crispy Fruit Spring Rolls

Prep: 10 mins | Cook: 10 mins | Serves: 4

Ingredients:

US: 8 spring roll wrappers, 2 bananas (sliced), 100g strawberries (sliced), 1 tablespoon honey, 1 teaspoon cinnamon UK: 8 spring roll wrappers, 2 bananas (sliced), 100g strawberries (sliced), 1 tablespoon honey, 1 teaspoon cinnamon

Instructions:

1. Preheat your Salter Air Fryer to 190°C (374°F).
2. Lay out the spring roll wrappers and place a few slices of banana and strawberry in the centre of each.
3. Drizzle with honey and sprinkle with cinnamon.
4. Fold the sides over the filling and roll up tightly.
5. Place the rolls in the air fryer basket, seam side down.
6. Cook for 8-10 minutes until golden brown and crispy.
7. Serve warm.

Nutritional Info: Calories: 150 | Fat: 2g | Carbs: 33g | Protein: 2g

Lemon Drizzle Cake Slices

Prep: 10 mins | Cook: 20 mins | Serves: 8

Ingredients:

US: 200g all-purpose flour, 150g granulated sugar, 1 teaspoon baking powder, 1/4 teaspoon salt, 2 eggs, 120ml milk, 60ml vegetable oil, 1 lemon (zested and juiced), 100g powdered sugar (for drizzle)

UK: 200g plain flour, 150g granulated sugar, 1 teaspoon baking powder, 1/4 teaspoon salt, 2 eggs, 120ml milk, 60ml vegetable oil, 1 lemon (zested and juiced), 100g icing sugar (for drizzle)

Instructions:

1. Preheat your Salter Air Fryer to 160°C (320°F).
2. In a bowl, mix flour, granulated sugar, baking powder, and salt.
3. In another bowl, whisk together eggs, milk, vegetable oil, lemon zest, and juice.
4. Pour the wet ingredients into the dry ingredients and mix until just combined.
5. Pour the batter into a greased air fryer-safe baking pan.
6. Cook for 18-20 minutes until a toothpick inserted into the centre comes out clean.
7. Let cool, then mix powdered sugar with lemon juice to make the drizzle.
8. Drizzle over the cooled cake before serving.

Nutritional Info: Calories: 200 | Fat: 8g | Carbs: 30g | Protein: 3g

Strawberry Shortcake Stacks

Prep: 10 mins | Cook: 10 mins | Serves: 4

Ingredients:

US: 200g strawberries (sliced), 120g all-purpose flour, 50g granulated sugar, 1 teaspoon baking powder, 1/4 teaspoon salt, 60g unsalted butter (cold and cubed), 60ml milk, 1 teaspoon vanilla extract, whipped cream (for serving) UK: 200g strawberries (sliced), 120g plain flour, 50g granulated sugar, 1 teaspoon baking powder, 1/4 teaspoon salt, 60g unsalted butter (cold and cubed), 60ml milk, 1 teaspoon vanilla extract, whipped cream (for serving)

Instructions:

Preheat your Salter Air Fryer to 180°C (356°F).

In a bowl, mix flour, sugar, baking powder, and salt.

Rub in the cold butter until the mixture resembles coarse crumbs.

Stir in milk and vanilla extract until just combined.

Drop spoonfuls of the dough onto a parchment-lined air fryer basket.

Cook for 10-12 minutes until golden brown.

Let cool, then slice the shortcakes in half.

Layer with sliced strawberries and whipped cream before serving.

Nutritional Info: Calories: 250 | Fat: 12g | Carbs: 32g | Protein: 3g

CHAPTER 10: SAUCES, DIPS, AND EXTRAS (15 RECIPES)

Garlic Aioli

Prep: 10 mins Cook: 0 mins Serves: 1 cup

Ingredients:

US: 200ml mayonnaise, 3 garlic cloves (minced), 1 tablespoon lemon juice, 1 teaspoon Dijon mustard, salt, pepper

UK: 200ml mayonnaise, 3 garlic cloves (minced), 1 tablespoon lemon juice, 1 teaspoon Dijon mustard, salt, pepper

Instructions:

1. In a bowl, combine the mayonnaise, minced garlic, lemon juice, and Dijon mustard.
2. Season with salt and pepper to taste.
3. Mix until smooth and well combined.
4. Serve immediately or refrigerate until needed.

Nutritional Info: Calories: 90 Fat: 10g Carbs: 1g Protein: 0g

Spicy Sriracha Mayo

Prep: 5 mins Cook: 0 mins Serves: 1 cup

Ingredients:

US: 200ml mayonnaise, 2 tablespoons Sriracha sauce, 1 tablespoon lime juice, 1 teaspoon garlic powder, salt

UK: 200ml mayonnaise, 2 tablespoons Sriracha sauce, 1 tablespoon lime juice, 1 teaspoon garlic powder, salt

Instructions:

1. In a bowl, mix the mayonnaise, Sriracha sauce, lime juice, and garlic powder.
2. Season with salt to taste.
3. Stir until well blended.
4. Serve immediately or chill until needed.

Nutritional Info: Calories: 95 Fat: 11g Carbs: 1g Protein: 0g

Homemade Tomato Ketchup

Prep: 10 mins Cook: 30 mins Serves: 2 cups

Ingredients:

US: 800g canned tomatoes, 50g brown sugar, 60ml apple cider vinegar, 1 teaspoon salt, 1/2 teaspoon onion powder, 1/2 teaspoon garlic powder, 1/4 teaspoon allspice

UK: 800g canned tomatoes, 50g brown sugar, 60ml apple cider vinegar, 1 teaspoon salt, 1/2 teaspoon onion powder, 1/2 teaspoon garlic powder, 1/4 teaspoon allspice

Instructions:

1. In a saucepan, combine all the ingredients.
2. Bring to a boil over medium heat, then reduce to a simmer.
3. Cook for 30 minutes, stirring occasionally, until thickened.
4. Blend the mixture until smooth using an immersion blender or regular blender.
5. Allow to cool before transferring to a jar.
6. Store in the fridge for up to 2 weeks.

Nutritional Info: Calories: 20 Fat: 0g Carbs: 5g Protein: 1g

Honey Mustard Dip

Prep: 5 mins Cook: 0 mins Serves: 1 cup

Ingredients:

US: 100ml mayonnaise, 50ml Dijon mustard, 50ml honey, 1 tablespoon lemon juice
UK: 100ml mayonnaise, 50ml Dijon mustard, 50ml honey, 1 tablespoon lemon juice

Instructions:

1. In a bowl, whisk together the mayonnaise, Dijon mustard, honey, and lemon juice.
2. Mix until smooth and well combined.
3. Serve immediately or refrigerate until needed.

Nutritional Info: Calories: 70 Fat: 5g Carbs: 6g Protein: 0g

Sweet Chili Sauce

Prep: 5 mins Cook: 10 mins Serves: 1 cup

Ingredients:

US: 200ml water, 100g sugar, 60ml rice vinegar, 2 tablespoons chilli flakes, 1 tablespoon garlic (minced), 1 tablespoon cornstarch, 2 tablespoons water (for cornstarch slurry)

UK: 200ml water, 100g sugar, 60ml rice vinegar, 2 tablespoons chilli flakes, 1 tablespoon garlic (minced), 1 tablespoon cornstarch, 2 tablespoons water (for cornstarch slurry)

Instructions:

1. In a saucepan, combine water, sugar, rice vinegar, chilli flakes, and minced garlic.
2. Bring to a boil over medium heat, stirring occasionally.
3. In a small bowl, mix cornstarch with water to create a slurry.
4. Slowly add the slurry to the saucepan, stirring constantly until the sauce thickens.
5. Remove from heat and let cool.
6. Store in a jar and refrigerate for up to 2 weeks.

Nutritional Info: Calories: 50 Fat: 0g Carbs: 12g Protein: 0g

Tzatziki Sauce

Prep: 10 mins Cook: 0 mins Serves: 1 cup

Ingredients:

US: 200g Greek yoghurt, 1 cucumber (grated and drained), 2 garlic cloves (minced), 1 tablespoon lemon juice, 1 tablespoon olive oil, 1 teaspoon dill (chopped), salt, pepper

UK: 200g Greek yoghurt, 1 cucumber (grated and drained), 2 garlic cloves (minced), 1 tablespoon lemon juice, 1 tablespoon olive oil, 1 teaspoon dill (chopped), salt, pepper

Instructions:

1. In a bowl, combine Greek yoghurt, grated cucumber, minced garlic, lemon juice, olive oil, and dill.
2. Season with salt and pepper to taste.
3. Mix until well combined.
4. Serve immediately or refrigerate until needed.

Nutritional Info: Calories: 40 Fat: 2g Carbs: 3g Protein: 3g

Barbecue Sauce

Prep: 10 mins Cook: 20 mins Serves: 2 cups

Ingredients:

US: 400g tomato sauce, 100g brown sugar, 60ml apple cider vinegar, 2 tablespoons Worcestershire sauce, 1 tablespoon mustard, 1 tablespoon smoked paprika, 1 teaspoon garlic powder, 1 teaspoon onion powder

UK: 400g tomato sauce, 100g brown sugar, 60ml apple cider vinegar, 2 tablespoons Worcestershire sauce, 1 tablespoon mustard, 1 tablespoon smoked paprika, 1 teaspoon garlic powder, 1 teaspoon onion powder

Instructions:

1. In a saucepan, combine all ingredients.
2. Bring to a boil over medium heat, then reduce to a simmer.
3. Cook for 20 minutes, stirring occasionally, until thickened.
4. Allow to cool before transferring to a jar.
5. Store in the fridge for up to 2 weeks.

Nutritional Info: Calories: 60 Fat: 0g Carbs: 15g Protein: 1g

Ranch Dressing

Prep: 5 mins Cook: 0 mins Serves: 1 cup

Ingredients:

US: 200ml buttermilk, 100g mayonnaise, 1 teaspoon garlic powder, 1 teaspoon onion powder, 1 teaspoon dried dill, 1 teaspoon dried parsley, salt, pepper

UK: 200ml buttermilk, 100g mayonnaise, 1 teaspoon garlic powder, 1 teaspoon onion powder, 1 teaspoon dried dill, 1 teaspoon dried parsley, salt, pepper

Instructions:

1. In a bowl, whisk together buttermilk, mayonnaise, garlic powder, onion powder, dill, and parsley.
2. Season with salt and pepper to taste.
3. Mix until smooth and well combined.
4. Serve immediately or refrigerate until needed.

Nutritional Info: Calories: 90 Fat: 9g Carbs: 2g Protein: 1g

Pesto Sauce

Prep: 10 mins Cook: 0 mins Serves: 1 cup

Ingredients:

US: 50g fresh basil leaves, 30g pine nuts, 50g Parmesan cheese (grated), 2 garlic cloves, 100ml olive oil, salt, pepper

UK: 50g fresh basil leaves, 30g pine nuts, 50g Parmesan cheese (grated), 2 garlic cloves, 100ml olive oil, salt, pepper

Instructions:

1. In a food processor, combine basil leaves, pine nuts, Parmesan cheese, and garlic.
2. Pulse until finely chopped.
3. With the processor running, slowly add the olive oil until smooth.
4. Season with salt and pepper to taste.
5. Serve immediately or store in a jar and refrigerate for up to 1 week.

Nutritional Info: Calories: 100 Fat: 10g Carbs: 1g Protein: 2g

Salsa Verde

Prep: 10 mins Cook: 0 mins Serves: 1 cup

Ingredients:

US: 200g tomatillos (husked and chopped), 1/2 onion (chopped), 1 garlic clove, 1 jalapeño (chopped), 1 lime (juiced), 30g fresh coriander (chopped), salt

UK: 200g tomatillos (husked and chopped), 1/2 onion (chopped), 1 garlic clove, 1 jalapeño (chopped), 1 lime (juiced), 30g fresh coriander (chopped), salt

Instructions:

1. In a blender, combine tomatillos, onion, garlic, jalapeño, lime juice, and coriander.
2. Blend until smooth.
3. Season with salt to taste.
4. Serve immediately or refrigerate until needed.

Nutritional Info: Calories: 20 Fat: 0g Carbs: 5g Protein: 1g

Tartar Sauce

Prep: 10 mins Cook: 0 mins Serves: 1 cup

Ingredients:

US: 200ml mayonnaise, 50g pickles (finely chopped), 1 tablespoon capers (chopped), 1 tablespoon lemon juice, 1 teaspoon Dijon mustard, salt, pepper

UK: 200ml mayonnaise, 50g pickles (finely chopped), 1 tablespoon capers (chopped), 1 tablespoon lemon juice, 1 teaspoon Dijon mustard, salt, pepper

Instructions:

1. In a bowl, mix mayonnaise, chopped pickles, capers, lemon juice, and Dijon mustard.
2. Season with salt and pepper to taste.
3. Stir until well combined.
4. Serve immediately or refrigerate until needed.

Nutritional Info: Calories: 90 Fat: 9g Carbs: 2g Protein: 0g

Hummus

Prep: 10 mins Cook: 0 mins Serves: 2 cups

Ingredients:

US: 400g canned chickpeas (drained), 2 tablespoons tahini, 2 garlic cloves (minced), 2 tablespoons lemon juice, 60ml olive oil, 1/2 teaspoon cumin, salt, pepper

UK: 400g canned chickpeas (drained), 2 tablespoons tahini, 2 garlic cloves (minced), 2 tablespoons lemon juice, 60ml olive oil, 1/2 teaspoon cumin, salt, pepper

Instructions:

1. In a food processor, blend chickpeas, tahini, minced garlic, lemon juice, olive oil, cumin, salt, and pepper until smooth.
2. If too thick, add a little water while blending until the desired consistency is reached.
3. Taste and adjust seasoning if needed.
4. Serve immediately or refrigerate in a sealed container.

Nutritional Info: Calories: 150 Fat: 10g Carbs: 12g Protein: 5g

Guacamole

Prep: 10 mins Cook: 0 mins Serves: 1 cup

Ingredients:

US: 2 ripe avocados, 1 tomato (seeded and diced), 1/4 onion (finely chopped), 1 garlic clove (minced), 1/2 lime (juiced), 1 tablespoon fresh coriander (chopped), salt, pepper

UK: 2 ripe avocados, 1 tomato (seeded and diced), 1/4 onion (finely chopped), 1 garlic clove (minced), 1/2 lime (juiced), 1 tablespoon fresh coriander (chopped), salt, pepper

Instructions:

1. Scoop out the flesh of the avocados into a bowl and mash with a fork.
2. Add diced tomato, finely chopped onion, minced garlic, lime juice, and chopped coriander.
3. Season with salt and pepper to taste.
4. Mix until well combined.
5. Serve immediately with tortilla chips or as a topping for dishes.

Nutritional Info: Calories: 120 Fat: 10g Carbs: 8g Protein: 2g

Caramelized Onions

Prep: 5 mins Cook: 30 mins Serves: 1 cup

Ingredients:

US: 4 large onions (sliced), 30g butter, 2 tablespoons olive oil, 1 tablespoon brown sugar, salt, pepper

UK: 4 large onions (sliced), 30g butter, 2 tablespoons olive oil, 1 tablespoon brown sugar, salt, pepper

Instructions:

1. Heat butter and olive oil in a large pan over medium heat.
2. Add sliced onions and cook, stirring occasionally, for about 20 minutes until the onions are soft and translucent.
3. Sprinkle brown sugar over the onions and continue to cook for another 10 minutes, stirring occasionally, until the onions are golden brown and caramelized.
4. Season with salt and pepper to taste.
5. Remove from heat and let cool slightly before serving.

Nutritional Info: Calories: 150 Fat: 10g Carbs: 15g Protein: 2g

Roasted Garlic

Prep: 5 mins Cook: 30 mins Serves: 1 bulb

Ingredients:

US: 1 bulb of garlic, 1 tablespoon olive oil, salt, pepper

UK: 1 bulb of garlic, 1 tablespoon olive oil, salt, pepper

Instructions:

1. Preheat the oven to 180°C (350°F).
2. Peel away the outer layers of the garlic bulb skin, leaving the skins of the individual cloves intact.
3. Using a knife, cut off 1/4 to a 1/2 inch of the top of the cloves, exposing the individual cloves of garlic.
4. Place the garlic heads in a baking dish. Drizzle with olive oil and season with salt and pepper.
5. Cover with aluminum foil.
6. Bake for 30-35 minutes, or until the cloves feel soft when pressed.
7. Allow to cool before squeezing the garlic from the skins.

Nutritional Info: Calories: 30 Fat: 2g Carbs: 3g Protein: 1g

MEASUREMENT AND CONVERSION CHART

VOLUME CONVERSIONS

Metric	Imperial	US
5 ml	1 teaspoon	1 teaspoon
15 ml	1 tablespoon	1 tablespoon
60 ml	2 fl oz	1/4 cup
120 ml	4 fl oz	1/2 cup
240 ml	8 fl oz	1 cup
1 litre	1.76 pints	4.23 cups

WEIGHT CONVERSIONS

Metric	Imperial
28 g	1 oz

100 g	3.5 oz
225 g	8 oz (1/2 lb)
450 g	16 oz (1 lb)
1 kg	2.2 lbs

TEMPERATURE CONVERSIONS

Celsius	Fahrenheit	Gas Mark
150°C	300°F	2
160°C	320°F	3
180°C	350°F	4
190°C	375°F	5
200°C	400°F	6
220°C	425°F	7

COMMON INGREDIENT CONVERSIONS

Flour
1 cup = 120 g
1/2 cup = 60 g
1/4 cup = 30 g

Sugar (granulated)
1 cup = 200 g
1/2 cup = 100 g
1/4 cup = 50 g

Butter
1 cup = 225 g
1/2 cup = 115 g
1/4 cup = 60 g

Liquids (water, milk, oil)
1 cup = 240 ml
1/2 cup = 120 ml
1/4 cup = 60 ml

Handy Equivalents
1 medium onion = about 110 g chopped
1 medium potato = about 150 g
1 medium carrot = about 60 g
1 large egg = about 60 g

1 cup grated cheese = about 100 g

AIR FRYER-SPECIFIC TIPS

When converting traditional recipes to air fryer:
- Reduce temperature by 25°C (50°F)
- Reduce cooking time by 20-25%
- Use about 75% less oil

CHECKING FOR DONENESS:

- Use a meat thermometer for precise results
- Internal temperature for chicken: 75°C (165°F)
- Internal temperature for beef (medium): 60°C (140°F)

CONCLUSION

As we come to the end of this cookbook, I hope you're feeling inspired and ready to embark on your air frying journey with your Salter appliance. Let's recap some of the key points we've covered:

WHAT WE'VE LEARNED

The basics of air frying technology and how it can transform your cooking

Essential techniques for getting the most out of your Salter Air Fryer

A wide range of delicious recipes, from quick snacks to full meals

Important safety guidelines and maintenance advice

The Air Frying Advantage

Remember, your Salter air fryer isn't just another kitchen gadget – it's a versatile tool that can help you:

Cook healthier meals with less oil

Save time and energy in the kitchen

Achieve crispy, delicious results without the hassle of deep frying

Experiment with a variety of cuisines and cooking styles

Moving Forward

As you begin to use your air fryer more frequently, you'll develop your tips and tricks. Don't be afraid to experiment and make recipes your own. Some suggestions to keep your air frying journey exciting:

1. Start a cooking journal: Note down your successes, areas for improvement, and any modifications you make to recipes.

2. Join air fryer communities: There are many online forums and social media groups where you can share experiences and get new ideas.

3. Challenge yourself: Try a new recipe or ingredient each week to expand your air frying repertoire.

4. Get the family involved: Air frying can be a fun activity for the whole family. Let everyone choose a recipe or create their combinations.

FINAL THOUGHTS

Cooking should be enjoyable, and your Salter air fryer is here to make it easier and more fun. Don't worry if your first few attempts aren't perfect – like any skill, air frying improves with practice. Remember the tips and techniques we've discussed, refer back to the recipes and conversion charts when needed, and most importantly, have fun in the kitchen.

Thank you for joining me on this air-frying adventure. Here's to many delicious, crispy, and healthier meals in your future. Happy air frying.

Bon appétit.

Printed in Great Britain
by Amazon